YOU'RE ALREADY
ALREADY
Awesome

YOU'RE ALREADY Awesome

HOW TO SILENCE YOUR INNER CRITIC AND STEP INTO GREATNESS

Alison Faulkner

HarperOne
An Imprint of HarperCollinsPublishers

HarperCollins books may be purchased for educational, business, or sales promotional use. For information, please email the Special Markets Department at SPsales@harpercollins.com.

FIRST EDITION

Designed by SBI Book Arts, LLC

Library of Congress Cataloging-in-Publication Data has been applied for.

ISBN 978-0-06-307596-2

22 23 24 25 26   LSC   10 9 8 7 6 5 4 3 2 1

To the one who is at their breaking point,
and to all those who support and
lift others who have hit theirs.

For Julie, who came down in the hole,
sat with me, made me laugh, believed me
and believed in me, and then helped
me and this book find our way out.

Oh, and to the one, the only, the talented,
the sexy, and the sensational magician
of music and creator of aura-bending tunes,
my husband, Mr. Eric Robertson!
I love you more.

Spent years doubting myself.
I'm done with that now.

—NAKEIA HOMER

CONTENTS

YOU'RE ALREADY ALREADY

Awesome

Feel Awesome Now

Hello, I'm Alison. I'm really superexcited you are here. I think the best way to introduce myself, which seems necessary because we're about to have a lengthy conversation in book form, is to do it the way I do it when I'm speaking to an audience that I've been hired to speak to, which is something I regularly do.

So let's set the scene. I want you to imagine a very average-looking, and I do mean average, as in average height, average weight (I'm 100 percent serious; I am the exact average in the US), white-blond white lady in her thirties in a pseudoprofessional but also very loud outfit. Imagine her, which is me, slowly climbing the stairs to a stage, while air humping, thrusting, and maybe adding a bit of a spin, to a song that will either make you immediately like me more or cause you to question if you should skip this thing entirely. Let's say James Brown's "Get Up Offa That Thing!" I will enthusiastically shimmy onto stage, take a moment to catch my breath, and then tell a brief anecdote that will connect us. For example, in this case I might say, "Isn't starting a new book exciting? I know I love starting a new book!

I always hope it will do what I want it to do!" And then I do a sort of transition and say, "So it's awesome we both like starting new books, but who am I, right?! Why did anyone hire ME to speak to you?"

Then I whip out the big guns and show you my first slide. It has an illustration of my head wearing large sunglasses. This tells you a lot. It tells you: This woman has commissioned and paid someone to illustrate her face. She seems to like sunglasses.

And then next to my animated floating head is the caption:
    I am not totally sane.

I'm not entirely sure how most audiences respond to this, even though I've done it dozens of times. I'm not entirely sure because I'm personally so amused by it every single time, I don't notice if anyone else is. And before anyone has too much time to become uncomfortable I follow it quickly with slide number 2, which says:

But I am awesome.

And I believe you're awesome too.

Okay, we're back in the book now, and here's what I mean by "awesome." Yes, I was born in Southern California and have been accused of having a Valley girl accent, but I don't mean awesome in a gum-popping, airbrushed-on-a-surfboard kind of way. I mean it in the way that you are full of "awe." Awe being a quiet reverent respect. And why are you full of awe? Why are you so insanely and inherently awesome?

Because your existence in every single moment is a phenomenon. A miracle. There is no other entity with your combination of experiences, genes, timing, relationships, ideas, and awareness. You are a creation of infinite potential and growth. That is AWESOME.

COME ON! THAT IS AWESOME.

You can literally choose to think anything. Like try it, think "anything." Say it in your head. That is crazy! Who is doing that?! How does that happen? You didn't even have to try. You just knew how to do it! And who, by the way, is doing it? It can't be your mind, your brain, because then who is observing it? Who observed you saying "anything"? What part of you is that? Gary Zukav calls it the Seat of the Soul; I like that one. Some call it spirit; quantum physics calls it energy. Pantheism calls it nature. The current spiritual movement mostly calls it Universe. Many call it God. Michael Singer, who often asks people in his books and lectures to say "hello" over and over in their mind, says, "There is nothing more important to true growth than realizing that you are not the voice of the mind; you are the one who hears it." So YOU are the one who hears the voice.

Listen, we don't have to be rocket scientists to feel it. That we are not the voice of the mind, we are the one who hears it.[1] And that one is without form, and so freaking limitless. And that is the real you. And you are awesome.

So maybe you're thinking, *Cute, Alison. You seem really excited about me being a miracle and limitless. And I might even want to agree with some of these ideas, but why does it matter?*

Here's why it matters to me.

Because no matter how it manifests in your life, most of us, most of the time, are operating from a lie. It's the same lie that continues to compound our suffering, no matter how we feel it, what words we use to describe it, or what we feel caused it.

And the lie is this: Our value is measured by the value we create and the value that others give us. That we have to "earn" or "prove" our value. That we are not inherently worthy, enough, or even just okay. And in order to be "okay" we need people, places, and things that are all outside of ourselves and most likely only gained through pain. THIS IS A LIE.

Hustle culture, which I define as the idea that your worth and value lay outside yourself and that you must constantly be bettering yourself and striving to be more, is so predominant, so sneakily oozing from underneath almost every message we hear, that we have the word *hustle* embroidered on pillows at big-box craft stores. You've got your ribbon, yarn, fake florals, and decorative throws encouraging their target demographic of fifty-year-old women to hustle for their worth. And we don't bat an eye at it.

I used to live in all-consuming sheer panic and anxiety that there was something more I could be doing and should be doing at all times. And I was pretty sure that whatever I was doing, I was doing it wrong or it didn't feel like it was supposed to feel.

I used to operate from a place of certainty that my best would never be enough, it could never be enough, and that despite sincerely giving a whole effort each day I would always somehow come up short.

I used to scurry around taking action from a place of thinking that to be good, which was of the utmost importance to me, I had to allow anyone who needed anything from me—my energy, my joy, my skill—to take it. I believed this because I am incredibly blessed, privileged, and have a lot of good things in my life. And I believed that if I didn't do this I was being selfish.

Living like this for so many years taught my body how to suppress almost any emotion other than anxiety, panic, and fear. I learned early on that from a place of anxiety I could get a lot done. And getting lots done made me feel good and valuable. Adrenaline fueled my body and I could work for hours and hours with no sleep. Completely blocking out any physical needs, ignoring pains and urges. Except the one for Diet Coke.

The craziest part about all this is I used to think this meant that I was doing a "good job" because I wasn't thinking about myself. I was working and doing and serving! But in reality it was completely selfish because all this tired, frantic, painful action was stemming from a place of wanting to control how others perceived me. And not just how others perceived me but, really, how I perceived myself.

How do I know this? Because I felt exhausted and drained. You *can* live in service and do great things, without feeling so drained, but that's not what I was doing.

Mind you, I did all this, and operated this way, all while moving nicely through the world. I married a wonderful man, had three children, created and ran my own businesses. It's not like I was miserable every hour of every day. I was very happy a lot! It's not like I was pretending the joy, passion, enthusiasm, love, hope, and faith I also felt. All those beliefs, that panic, that anxiety, it coexisted with a very lovely life. But it also just about killed me. I just about killed myself.

And I really do mean that. On many occasions, l have shared that I feel like I should die, or rather not be allowed to live, when I fall short of what I DECIDE my best is. Ceasing to exist pops up as a viable option in my mind when I "fail" or make a mistake. This might sound severe to you, but it's my reality. And at those few times I have been brave enough to share it, people close to me, doctors, nurses, family—they laugh in my face. They actually laugh. Out of nervousness, out of disbelief. It hurts. It really hurts. It made me think my pain was a joke. And I used to laugh, too, to make others feel comfortable. I laughed to make it seem smaller or less serious. I don't anymore. Living and believing this lie truly almost cost me my life. And I know I'm not alone.

But I have good news! I no longer believe the lie that I'm inherently wrong, flawed, need correction, or have to live my life in a way to prove and be perceived as "good." I no longer feel it in my bones, my skin, my body. Well, that's not entirely true, I often still feel it. BUT I KNOW it's a lie. I recognize it before I internalize it. I can see the lie as it pops its beady little head up over and over in my mind, Whac-A-Mole style. I also no longer operate from it.

I know the truth is this:

I am awesome. And if I am awesome, everyone else is too.

In fact, I now see it's inhumane to believe that I am unworthy or less than another person. Because if I believe it to be true for myself, I have to apply it to those around me. And then what am I doing? Ranking and ordering divine creatures? How dare I! The state of the country, the world, and the annals of history have shown us the devastating effects of ranking and valuing one life over another.

So here's what I want to do: I want to explore how we can feel awesome now. Rather than just crappy. I'm going to talk to you about what *feel awesome now* really means. And share with you how I do it, using my experiences, which is all I have, the things I've learned that help me, and the experiences of thousands of people I've shared these ideas with, coached, and learned this with along the way.

But I Don't Feel Awesome

If we are so awesome, why do we feel so bad?

Good question. I'm glad you asked. I have been obsessed with it for almost my entire life.

Short answer: you keep forgetting what you actually are. Who you actually are.

Why? Because like a flower, and the Macarena, it's both insanely simple and miraculously complex.

You are consciousness, love, light, awareness, spirit, energy, God, nature, Universe, the witness—pick your poison! There's no word for it because it's so big! And there's every word for it because it's so big! Which is why for the purposes of this book I'll use lots of words, but mostly *awesome*.

If we can't agree on that yet (which I'm fine with), let's at least lock this one in: you are not your thoughts. You are the one who hears. That one is formless. And because we live in a world of form, we just keep getting confused. And you thinking that you are your thoughts, your actions, your results, your form, that is what is making you feel like crap.

By claiming you can, always at any point, choose to feel awesome now, I'm not saying you are like a robot who is supposed to feel what we've decided are positive emotions at all times. There will be suffering. There will be pain. It's part of the awesome.

(And yes, I know the grammatically correct way to say this would be "awesomeness," but it's my party and I'll use words how I want to!) Back to your awesome (n.).

Let me tell you about our dog Spike. Spike is an anxious, fickle little Jack Russell terrier and he doesn't like typical dog things like playing fetch or chew toys. He likes to pace around the house, steal food, snuggle under mounds of heavy blankets for hours on end, and have the constant attention of my husband. Spike and I have a lot in common. I like to think it's why my husband, Eric, chose to adopt him and loves him so much!

Like many small, yappy dogs, Spike loses his tiny mind and barks up a storm when someone comes to the door. We've worked on this with a trainer and he's better about it when Eric is around, but he has little respect for me and is terrible when it's just the two of us. And while it's often infuriating to try to answer the door and interact with a guest while Spike sounds his canine alarm, it's objectively hysterical that this twelve-pound-nothing believes he's protecting us from all possible threats.

Your thoughts, our minds—well, they are Spike. Yapping and yapping, thinking they can control the outside world, keep us safe, and predict what will happen. Our thoughts are just as futile, if not more so, than that pint-size terrier. And our thoughts and what we choose to focus on can make us feel awful. They trick us into forgetting our awesome.

To try to ease my lifelong anxiety I've learned a lot. I've learned how we can change our thoughts to change our lives. I learned that thoughts contribute to feelings, and some thoughts serve and expand us while others do not. And this is all 100 percent true! Be positive! Be grateful! We'll show you all the science that supports it! And they did, and I did. And it kind of works.

But somewhere along the line I started to believe that the goal was to control my thoughts. That the goal was to have all the right or correct thoughts to get all the things and outcomes I wanted. When this didn't totally work, I thought I should get really Zen and have no thoughts. I think a lot of us stop there. We feel miserable and like failures for having the same "wrong" thoughts or not being able to YAP the "right" ones loudly enough. We try to meditate because everyone says it will make us feel good, but we feel worse because we can't do it "right." We can't stop thinking!

I can now see that trying to control our thoughts is like putting a tampon in a gun wound. It will temporarily stop the bleeding, which is great, but ultimately do nothing to address the root issue.

Where am I going with this? After doing some research, Eric told me that Spike yapping at the front door was just part of his nature. He's doing it to protect us. God bless him. So we should quickly thank him for doing his job, acknowledge him—throw him a bone if you will—and then tell him, all is well. You did your job, little puppy, thank you for the alarm, I'll check it out. Yup, all is well.

My anxious energy, my self-doubt, and my predictions of how everyone will hate me—you know those thoughts, right? I don't let them yap and yap and yap anymore. Well, I try not to, although sometimes they still get pretty loud. But now I work on noticing them, and thanking them for trying to keep me safe, rather than telling them to automatically shut up or not happen.

After I notice the thoughts, I try to, as Terror Squad featuring Fat Joe and Remy Ma said in their 2004 hit "Lean Back":

"And do the rockaway, now lean back, lean back, lean back, lean back." But lean back into what? You guessed it. My inner knowing, my intuition, my soul, my presence, my awesome.

You feel like crap not because you are crap but because life is hard.

Life is difficult! Our bodies have pain and people do and say awful things. We do and say awful things. I lived through 2020 too; we all had different experiences and circumstances, but I was there, and it sucked, oh baby it sucked. Yes?!

We don't feel awesome for a myriad of reasons. And this entire book will give you some techniques and lots of ideas to help you feel less crappy. But regardless of whether or not you read them, or even use them, the good news is you do not have to be an isolated victim of your thoughts anymore. You are not your thoughts. And you might feel like crap, but you are not crap. You are awesome.

My Awesome Invitation

In this book over and over I will invite you back to your center with the invitation that you can feel awesome now. This is not some insane claim that you will feel bliss twenty-four hours a day, or that positive emotions are the only emotions we should have. No shoulds!

The invitation is a call to remember your true nature. When you feel like garbage and forget, I want to create a positive feedback loop of remembrance. So we don't beat ourselves up and go, *Oh, I feel like crap again! I must be doing life wrong and find something else to do!* No. We've had enough of that. What we need is more kindness, more comfort, more nurturing. And that starts with kindness within ourselves. When you feel terrible, the invitation to feel awesome now can give you relief.

To ask yourself to even attempt to feel awesome signifies there is a part of you that WANTS to return to Truth. The Truth that you are AWESOME, you are a miracle, you are the witness, you are awareness, and you are so much bigger and greater than you know. Learning to feel awesome now is a focus that invites perspective. It turns your heart and mind to your Truth and offers the question, "What is this moment asking me to let go, learn, or pass through? What lie do I need to release so that I can feel and know my awesome?" It is a practice.

And what will the practice do for you? Everything. That thing you think you want, you'll realize you might not need it, that you already have it, or that it is absolutely on its way, without you having to be miserable.

But more specifically, here's what knowing my awesomeness, and more importantly operating from it, rather than operating from my mind, has done for me. Since I've been able to quiet my mind and anxiety I can see the world. Mother Earth in all her glory. Father Sky. I can feel the energy and wisdom of the ancient redwoods when I wrap my arms around them. I can see the dewdrops on leaves in the mountains and it fills me with wonder and peace. I feel connection and emotions in the people around me in a way that seems otherworldly. A new plane of existence has opened up.

The artist inside me (you have one too!), the artist I unintentionally squashed and drowned with criticism and fear, SHE has burst forth. I am creator, I am an artist unleashed! Or as I like to scream, "I AM A FREE AGENT OF CHAOS!" The miracle is I now can find JOY in the process of creation, not just joy or relief in the result. Our inner artist is so much a part of our inner child. This practice heals both. Claiming and knowing my divine awesomeness has healed horrific wounds I am now able to see and know. I am healed and healing.

I'm able to talk to people without needing to download and replay every moment of it afterward. I'm able to acknowledge mistakes and not feel the need to die. I'm able to do the biggest, scariest things I've only ever dreamed of before, like write a book.

I don't operate from the lie that I need to constantly be doing, and figuring, and earning my goodness and worth anymore, and I'm so much happier! I operate from these beliefs instead: that there are miracles and a caring and loving higher power that guides and directs us and longs for our elevated expansion and divine success.

I operate from a place of knowing that we can tap into that love, that power and flow IN ANY INSTANT and that by doing so we will be encircled in that ever-present love and be guided to serve the world in our highest capacity. I believe I can do this imperfectly and I'm still okay. I don't need to do anything perfectly because my core is perfect. What a relief!

I'm able to take action and be guided by gratitude, forgiveness, and change. I can see they are possible, and that all, yes, all—even me—are worthy and capable of giving and receiving love and forgiveness. That each human on this earth has come from greatness, has greatness within them, and can share and extend love and greatness.

I believe that we can be angels on earth. And that we can use our divine, unique talents, passions, difficult circumstances, weaknesses, and strengths to contribute to the world. I believe living that way IS living our purpose. And I believe that doing that and taking inspired love-fueled action is what will create positive lasting change. Inspired action feels almost effortless. I still believe in effort and work, but not force and shame.

I've been learning and beginning to understand that I can operate from this glorious place, know all these uplifting truths, and still feel like crap. You will still doubt yourself, you'll still feel fear, suffering, loneliness, and shame. BUT it's different; it doesn't last as long or cut as deep. It doesn't feel so personal. Because it's not. Because it means nothing about me and you. They're just emotions passing through.

Unfortunately, after much experimentation I've also seen that good intentions and taking inspired action cannot keep you safe from making harmful mistakes, and this practice will not keep others from disagreeing with and disliking you. This almost made me want to give up on the whole living-from-my-awesome operating system.

But I noticed that when I disappoint someone now, instead of that leading me to believe it's a good idea to jump off a balcony, an idea I've had more than once, I can sit with and witness the discomfort, without the need to run from it. It's okay to disappoint someone because of everything else I know. That we are worthy, we are forgivable, we can change, and in the end, the goal is not to please everyone. But to become the highest, most love-filled expanded versions of ourselves possible. And we can, with our awesomeness, extend that love and understanding to all, regardless of what is extended back to you. No self-flagellation required.

We cannot hide from pain and suffering; they make our hearts expand and souls grow. However, I believe we can work to eliminate self-imposed suffering. I believe that freeing ourselves from the self-imposed suffering that control, fear, and separation generate brings us true, glorious, soul-bursting freedom.

It feels really, really good to live in this light.

At the end of the day it's not perfect or easy, but it's simple. I am awesome, and so are you.

This book is about the practice of feeling it. And not just feeling it, but feeling it NOW. Not after you've become some mythical unicorn creature who only experiences wonderful things and has immaculate thoughts. Boo! How boring! Nope.

If you want to be you, which is a battle in and of itself because of that lie I mentioned, the lie that you are not okay as you are. But if you HOPE being you is enough, or even want to hope, GET READY. If you're tired of thinking a better life is just one more change away, one more push away. If you're overwhelmed with having to figure everything out. If you're sick of not having anyone who understands you. If you are so exhausted from trying to achieve that goal you just can't seem to reach. If you're done wondering, is this how it's supposed to be? If you're done feeling crappy in many ways . . .

Then we're going to have a lot of fun.

I have a gift. My gift is that I know that you are capable of connecting to and FEELING your greatness. No matter how impossible it seems, I KNOW it is true. I believe in your awesomeness. I know, as I say at the end of every *Awesome with Alison* podcast episode, "Only you can be you, and you're already as awesome as you need to be."

Let me repeat. You don't have to do anything! Just surrender, allow, accept your awesome.

How? That's what we'll uncover in the rest of the book. This chapter covers the *why*; the next twelve chapters will cover the *how*. You need a SHIFT. A shift in perspective, a shift in thought, a shift of focus.

I'm going to give you twelve shifts. Each shift will help you return to love, and shift back into an awareness of your awesomeness. I use these shifts every day, often multiple times a day, to help return me to flow, to love, to my awesome.

The rest of this book consists of application. How you can apply your desire to feel awesome now in any situation. These shifts give you examples of how to do that. Look specifically for sections titled "TAP It Out" (more on that below), or "Prevent the Spiral" to hone in on the practical application and exercises.

Each of the twelve shifts is rooted in a deep principle, like surrender, perspective, self-acceptance, or presence. These principles are connected to and integral in returning to your highest self, the witness, your spirit, your awesome, whatever you deem it is. The shifts can be used like a mantra, or an invitation to return to your awesome, to love, to light.

Use whatever shift you need, for whatever sucky situation you find yourself in. There's no right or wrong. I hope that when you feel like you're not sure where else to turn, you flip through this book, read the bold headline of each shift, and find one that speaks to your soul. I pray it quiets your fears and helps you feel seen.

We're going to break the shifts down, one by one. I will give you a concept, hash it out with you, show you how to apply it with examples, and then give actionable takeaways. I created each shift to stand alone. Even if you feel frantic, panicked, or depressed, or in a state in which you can hardly function, you can grab this book and flip to a shift that will serve you. I wrote it that way because yes, this book is for everyone, but it's REALLY a book for the person hiding under their desk. I've been there so many times. In my closet sobbing, or buried in sadness beneath my covers. I've been there and if you will allow me, I can be there in spirit with you. I really care about you feeling even a tiny bit better.

I care because I've spent so much time feeling bad. Numb to the awesome, the beauty, the glory that was always sitting patiently inside of me. My intention is to help you feel better. Not artificial, just better, more awesome. To live your beautiful, unique life.

I believe that the world needs you to feel it more. Because the world needs you, showing up, doing your thing, being exactly who you are. Why? You can say it with me this time, because only you can be you.

The relief is this: You're already as awesome as you need to be.

This Won't Work for Me!

At this point you might be thinking, *This sounds great for some people, but I don't think it will work for me.* As I've worked through this with thousands of people I've spoken to, I've come across a few common objections I want to address here before we go too far.

Objection #1: Are you saying I have to believe in God to read this book, or to feel awesome?

My life experience, my upbringing, and the language I've been surrounded with identify that great force, that soul-expanding well of power and flow as God. To me God is a Heavenly Father and creator. I also believe in a Heavenly Mother. I am currently spending a lot of energy on understanding and feeling the presence of Goddess, working to feel and know the Divine Feminine. So of course, it is difficult for me, in some ways, to feel that great loving force and not identify it as God or Goddess. It's the paradigm that has been created through my experience. And my understanding of what and who "God" is grows daily.

But as for you! Are you going to be able to relate to this book if you don't feel the same?

I believe that your "highest self" is divine. But I also wrote this entire book with my friend Tanner in my heart. My intention is that he could read and find solace in this book without being too triggered. He has been deeply hurt by religion and the idea of God. I see and respect his experience. I know that words like *Heavenly Father* and *Christ* have been weaponized against him. I love him so much. I hope that he, and you, if this is part of your experience, will be able to connect to your divine awesomeness with my words even if we use them differently.

Because I am 100 percent positive that both God and I don't care what you call your AWESOME.

Objection #2: This sounds great but obviously won't work for me because . . .

You probably already *know* the truth and answers you need. But if you know them, why are you not applying them or believing them? Why aren't they working for YOU? Why are you thinking that believing you are awesome, knowing it, and operating from your awesome, can't enable you to feel peace and love, and live a life you can hardly fathom?

Because you don't know what you don't know.

I cannot tell you how often I hear someone ask, "How do I get more motivation!?" Holy hell. You do not need more motivation. You simply need a fuller understanding. You need to try to figure out what it is that you don't know. And we can only do this by first accepting that you do not know everything.

Here are some good thought indicators that you are two-stepping into an area where you will block yourself from more fully understanding something, or discovering something you don't know. Thoughts like:

> I already know that.
> This can't apply to me.
> I've already tried that.
> This won't work for me.
> I'm different because . . .

Yeah, but . . .

Game recognizes game. The reason I can call out anyone for thinking they know everything or already thinking they know it, or believing it won't apply to them, is because I think all those things too. The person who believes everything is an answer for them and they have something to truly learn from everyone is a rare exception.

As the Buddhist proverb says: You can never step in the same river twice.

This will work for you because you're a freaking genius creator. Solutions are on their way; let go of thinking you already know everything so they can show up.

Objection #3: This is selfish, self-centered drivel.

Drivel? I've always loved the word. Nonsense. I love it. It is drivel. Thoughts are mostly drivel. I hope to take nothing too seriously, other than your nonnegotiable worth. Selfish? Well, here's a quote I live by:

"Happy people don't kill their husbands, they just don't" (Elle Woods, *Legally Blonde*).

Why does it matter if you're happy? Why is it not selfish to feel awesome?

Because we reflect what we feel. Because when you feel content, or whole, or ease, or peace, you reflect that into all your interactions, your work, and your relationships.

When I feel happy, I want to burst open and share. But *happy* isn't really my word. My word is *awesome*. I love the word *awesome* because I love alliteration and my name is Alison. I love the word *awesome* because it is an extreme version of "happy." I love the idea of inducing actual "awe."

As Celie writes that Albert said to her in Alice Walker's *The Color Purple*, "The more I wonder, the more I love."

I think of that awe as reverence and acknowledgment for the present moment. And being in awe of the entirety of life that we can experience in a single second.

Here is my personal definition of *awesome* as it pertains to my life and how I want to feel. You are welcome to take it, modify it, dissect it, or question it.

Feeling awesome means I'm allowing and following joy and expansion and my inner enthusiasm. That I am connected to the core divine being that I am. That I am part of God and Goddess and Love, and they are always encouraging greater understanding and growth, and never ever speaking in shame.

In each moment I don't expect myself to feel a tizzy of frantic enthusiasm, but enthusiasm is absolutely a go-to emotion for me. Which is why this definition works for me so well. It also makes sense why anxiety is also a go-to emotion for me, because excitement and anxiety are stimulated in the same part of the brain.

Today, even when I feel at my absolute lowest, I sing my favorite line from Disney's *Moana* to my fiery, frantic fear-fueled thoughts, just as she did to the lava monster Te Kā, ". . . this does not define you."

And it will start to open up new pathways to peace in my mind and return me to my awesome. Even in sadness, pain, and suffering.

Maybe you don't want to feel awesome, perhaps for you it's all about peace. Maybe being happy makes your heart sing, maybe it's joy, or wholeness, being connected or supported. I think it's empowering and fun to try on words and see which ones light you up.

Absolutely none of it is selfish. Because when you feel these things, you finally get out of your head and connect with the world around you.

Objection #4: This ideology sounds super Western, or privileged, or narrow.

"A bird doesn't sing because it has an answer, it sings because it has a song."—Maya Angelou

All I have ever wanted is to write a book. I did the math, and with my podcast alone I've created the equivalent of ten books. I've written a calendar, a daily guided journal, half a dozen in-depth online courses, a ten-hour workshop with an accompanying hundred-page workbook, and a dozen keynotes. All the same length as, if not more than the length of, a book.

I've written years of blog posts and multiple books' worth of captions on Instagram. And yet? Why only now am I writing a book?

For this exact objection.

Essentially that my narrow, or Western, or privileged, or whatever unqualified part of me you want to identify was simply not allowed to write a book. What business do I have sharing, writing, speaking? I spent years believing that I hadn't suffered enough to write a book. I mean, why should I bother? We have Viktor Frankl's *Man's Search for Meaning*. We don't need to hear what I have to say. It took me years to realize that I was waiting. Waiting to suffer enough so that I would be qualified. How much suffering would ever be enough? What an awful thing to wait for.

And I can see how my rallying cry that I say at the end of every podcast episode and repeat to audiences over and over—"Only you can be you, and you're already as awesome as you need to be!"—is absolutely very Western in its ideology and centered on the individual. But I was born in America. It's my experience. And though the language might be Western, and centered on the self, it's simply an access point.

It's my access point for understanding that I am not that limited self, none of us are, and that we are all connected. Access to the whole through the self is in fact millions of people's access point. Millions of us have the collective experience of hearing a constant barrage of messages encouraging us to do more in order to be more. We've been fed the lie that our value as a person is equal to the value we create for the system that we need to fit into. So, yes, it might start as narrow, but I believe it goes wide. Wide and deep into transcendent universal truths. I've heard it said we don't learn truth, we remember it. That's what I hope to do. Not teach you something you don't know, just help you uncover and remember.

After spending so many years being ashamed of my own experience, feeling terrible that it was or is narrow or limited, I come back to this: we are all only experts at one thing—our experience. And regardless of what our experience is, most of us are walking around thinking it's incorrect. That in some way, through either our fault or the fault of someone or something else, it's no good.

My experience is in so many ways one of incredible ease. A straight, cisgender, able-bodied, white female. The world, its systems, and society have been set up in my favor in a way that I know I'm only starting to scrape the surface of seeing. My whole life I have felt guilt for this. Why was I given so much when others were given so little? And I felt guilt for any sort of suffering I felt, because I should just appreciate my nice life and stop being so dramatic. Right?

But here's a technique I use often. I'll ask: How does this thought serve me? How did this thought, that my suffering or pain was indulgent and insignificant, serve those around me? Did it help me to get to a place where I could feel gratitude and peace and show up and serve with love?

No. Nope. It did not. It kept me in shame. It kept me in my pain. It kept me from seeking solutions and help.

So I share from my experience, which is all I have. I hope that from it I can do more good than harm. That I don't unintentionally reinforce narrow beliefs. I read, I listen; in the last six years specifically I've tried to seek out experiences that vary from my own very homogenous experience. I've been ignorant in the past of many things.

I know I cannot know your exact pain, your cross to bear; we might have wildly different experiences. And how beautiful that is. I still believe that the principles I share connect us, unite us, and empower us. I believe that we need many revolutions to combat the ailments of this world. The revolution I feel called to fight in is this one. The one of you realizing your greatness, your awesome, and being able to feel it. The revolution of being able to let go of the yapping thoughts that bark at you and distract you from your peace and power, and keep you from listening to your inner knowing. I hope to do this so that you can more clearly hear the battle cry of the cause that's calling you. And so when you hear it you feel brave enough, well enough, and strong enough to answer.

Because I just know it! I know you can bring peace to someone no one else can, because of your exact perfectly imperfect human experience. We need you to bring it, in the language you speak, exactly as you are. I hope to be one small link, connecting with other links in the chain of the love and beauty that is this marvelous, wondrous existence.

Objection #5: I'm too tired, overwhelmed, busy, or need more motivation to do this.

Good news. I am often too tired, overwhelmed, and frantic to be able to accept any more information. So this book and the twelve shifts I'm about to offer you all assume you are coming from the place of your breaking point.

If you're crying in your car, under your desk, in the corner of a bathroom or closet, I'm talking to you. I've thrown Queen Goddess Brené Brown's books across rooms because I felt so personally attacked by the suggestions. Ideas that if I had just kept reading might have saved me years of suffering. I love you, Brené. So I get it. I'm not here to demand anything of you. Simply offer some shifts to feel awesome now.

If you're a pretty high-functioning human, and just want a greater sense of ease and purpose, and all this crying in corners feels extreme, this is for you, too. One of my favorite drag queens, Alyssa Edwards, likes to say, "I don't get cute! I get drop-dead gorgeous!"

I modified this for my purpose and brand coaching by adding, "Insight is cute! But action is drop-dead gorgeous!"

I love to get cute with insight. But ultimately I want to be drop-dead gorgeous. So we will focus on how to take inspired, effortless action. How to align and live in the flow and take action from your awesome. It's very different from the exhausting kind of action you're probably used to.

So let's do this. You can do it. I believe in you. It's going to be fun.

TAP It Out!

I'm inviting you into these shifts, which I truly think could change your life, and we've covered that, objections aside, this book is for you. So let's start with some action. I believe the most powerful tool in this book is what I call my TAP method. When in doubt, TAP it out to feel awesome now! TAP stands for tune in, accept, and pick your focus. When you're feeling fear, anxiety, loneliness, hopelessness, a little bit snappy, drained, overwhelmed, or underwhelmed: TAP! Because I get that when you feel like crap, doing much of anything is a struggle.

So think of the TAP method as lifting a finger; it's the bare minimum for how to feel awesome now, just giving a little tap-a-roo. Just like how the tiny tap of one toe can ignite a body in dance, and give energy and joy to the bodies around it and invite them to dance! One tiny TAP from you can do the same. You don't even have to get up and learn a complicated fifteen-second routine; all you have to do, especially when you're feeling low, is TAP.

At the time of writing this I'm in St. George, Utah, alone in a little hotel room with about three weeks before my first book deadline. I have about 10 percent done. Yes. Yes. This is me.

I woke up and just felt awful. Logically, if I wanted to get all in my head about it, it made no sense. I'm not getting my period! I'm not sick, I have lots of good food, and I've been exercising. I went to bed feeling good and have had two solid days of usable writing. But I woke up and started doubting everything that I've written. I started to go to my same old stories, that my contribution isn't significant. That if I don't say the exact things that I should say, in the way I should say them, that I will get hate. Lots and lots of hate. That I will hurt people unintentionally and that I will cause more harm than good.

Obviously, I will be dragged down to hell with shame, and people won't listen to my message. And why should they? I should cancel the book deal. I still can, right? Right. And yes, this was this morning. I told you, I'm not a robot; I need what I teach, that's why I teach it. But basically I was just starting to spiral in fear.

I didn't want to write. I didn't want to do my morning meditations or yoga or mantras, none of that crap. I didn't want to get out of bed. So instead of praying, reading something uplifting, stretching, or exercising, I grabbed my phone and started scrolling. Oh, you betcha I hopped on Instagram and I started scrolling and scrolling. What on earth am I scrolling for?

I'm scrolling to get out of this uncomfortable feeling! I don't want to be here. I'm scrolling to get out of this doubt! I'm scrolling to get out of my skin, to change these thoughts! I'm scrolling for validation, for confirmation, perhaps for motivation?

Not surprisingly, I found absolutely none of those things. I just found more of what I was focusing on in the back of my brain: fear. After thirty seconds on social media, the anger felt bigger, the division felt wider. I felt more hopeless, less qualified, and less equipped, if possible, than I did before.

So I started to think, *What do I mean when I say, feel awesome now? Am I living it? Am I a fraud? Practice what you preach right now, right in this moment. Do it now.*

In preparation for this book I created a quick method. A shortcut to feel awesome now. I made an acronym because even though I consciously practice this all the time, I needed something memorable, quick, and cute. Because that's what social media is offering, and I need something that has a fighting chance.

It came to me in the bathtub, as so many good things do. *T* is for tune in. Not tune out to the world, out to social media, out to calling a friend and asking for validation. None of those things are inherently bad. But they are never the first step to feel awesome now. Tuning in, going in, that is.

So how did I choose to "tune in" this morning? I had one of my little Alison conversations.

My awesome: Hey, Alison, what's going on?

Frantic me: Um, I'm really convinced the world's problems are too big. I am afraid to share my truth. I'm positive everyone is going to hate me and it's all going to just be really awful.

My awesome: Okay, yeah. That sounds really scary. Let's tune in some more. What's the actual feeling? The emotion? Is it anxiety? Panic? Overwhelm?

Frantic me: Fear. It's fear. Fear that I'm not enough. Fear that my offering is stupid. Fear that it will be really, really painful when I fail.

Now, this seems simple. But honestly to tune in is one of the hardest things we can do. To objectively tune in like this, with an observational tone rather than identifying with the frantic voice. This has been a journey for me. Like most things I want to share, it's simple, but sometimes difficult, well, at least for me. To question the feeling of earth-shattering urgency, the emotion objectively, without falling into it so deep I can't get out.

I start to take for granted the work it took me to get to this point. But it doesn't have to take you that long. I think it will depend on your mental health, what other tools you need, if this is your first time doing something like this. So don't worry about it. This is simply a practice. Something that you choose to do. Something that you elect to do. And honestly, if I hadn't done it at this point, in another hour or two the emotions would've just compounded and it would've been even harder. Just know no matter where you are in your spiral, you can attempt to tune in and observe or question the chattering. The yapping dog.

Another technique I employed subconsciously was identifying if my emotions and thoughts were stemming from love or fear. The extreme nature of them made it pretty easy for me to tell. But I could ask, *Is this discomfort because I'm going to be expanded, and writing a book and sharing and opening myself up to lots of people is uncomfortable?* That discomfort is rooted in love. But I felt like crawling into a hole and dying. That is shame-based fear. That is lack fear—not a good type of discomfort—that expands; so, in this case, it wasn't an uncomfortable *I'm not sure what's going to happen!* but more of an *Everything that I love and everything that I think is good about myself everyone else is going to say is trash!*

Throughout the book I'll offer lots of ways to tune in. So let's move to the *A* in TAP.

A is for: accept. I did that like this.

> *My awesome:* Oh, hey, fear. Good to see you again.
> Thanks for trying to keep me safe.

Again! This seems so simple. But all the alternatives are what I used to do. And they kept me in this feeling of complete and utter panic.

Alternative (shame-induced) responses:

- Stop it! You shouldn't be feeling this way!

- We've been through this, you need to fight and force your way through it!

- It doesn't matter what other people think, you should do what you feel called to do; you know that and if you were truly an enlightened person, you wouldn't be worried about this!

- There are such bigger problems in the world! People are truly suffering and all you can do is be worried about your stupid little book?

⦿ Yes, you should quit! You should be afraid! You have a nice life right now, there's no need to change!

⦿ You're a good person doing good things and you don't need to expose yourself to all the haters out there in the world!

I could keep going endlessly. There are so many alternatives. And honestly, a lot of thought work and positive thinking techniques stay here and help you try to manage these thoughts. This is an awesome practice! It's what I did for years and we will do it too. But what it usually turns into is me trying to control my responses, trying to micromanage my thoughts. I of course still do it out of habit, but not this morning. Remember, this morning I practiced what I preach.

I did the *A* in TAP. I accepted.

What's your experience? What keeps you from accepting? What keeps you from knowing what you are feeling? Do you use numbing? Is it one dominant emotion you use like a drug? Is it drugs, a lack of drugs? Is it an unwillingness to see your hormones might need balancing or medical help? Again, don't stress; we've got the whole book to work through it.

But let me promise you this. You're never going to lovingly accept your uncomfortable feeling, thought, or emotion, and get stuck in it. It's like quicksand; the more you struggle, the faster you sink. The more you hold still, the more solutions appear.

But back to ME!

I accepted even deeper. I let frantic Alison do this, because she had more to say, as she usually does.

Frantic Alison: Yeah, I'm just trying to protect you. Yeah! This makes a lot of sense! And guess what, even if it makes no sense it's my truth so who cares! It's mine! Sit on it, share it, don't share it! I accept this fear and I don't have to do anything about it!

This is cute and fun and rebellious of me, but that's why there's step 3. The *P* in TAP.

And *P* is about minding your *P*s. Pick your focus! What focus? Maybe being present, being in your power, sitting in peace and looking at the process. But mostly focus on the present.

My awesome: Pick your focus. What's happening in the present? Notice it. Feel it.

Not-so-frantic Alison: Well, I'm in my bed. It's a really nice bed, actually a warm, safe bed. I'm in my bed and I mean, if I'm being honest, yesterday I wrote two huge chapters that at the time I thought were pretty good. I am safe in the present. I am loved in the present. I only have the present. My process was full of flow. Of light. Of awesome.

And then I felt it. I felt awesome. I caught a glimpse of my divinity, my presence, my awareness, my expansion.

I took a deep breath in. Exhaled. I felt the present moment in my body.

What happened next was not a thought process. It was presence. It's what I will call inspired action. Effortless action. You might recognize it as intuition, or flow. It's different from the constant stream of chattering thoughts. It's more of a feeling, it's more of a quiet suggestion.

Remember how I was in my bed for this? And though I've

drawn it out, it probably happened in minutes, maybe even one minute. After my TAP practice I noticed that I was getting out of bed. I noticed that I was brushing my teeth. I reached for my running shoes.

At that point I noticed my mind start to question the schedule of the day . . . I started to THINK. I thought, *Well, if I go running now, how much time will I have to write before it's time for lunch? And what time is the sun going to set? And maybe I should sit down and block out the day and . . .*

Just like that I was back to thought. So I TAPped it out again. I tuned in: I was wanting to control, thinking that if I just plan and plan everything will go the way I want! And then I accepted: I want control. That's okay, control is a fear response. Finally, I picked my focus: currently I am in flow—so I follow it, I trust. I don't really want control, even if it feels like I do. I want flow.

I trust this present moment because it feels effortless, it feels beautiful, and it's moving toward something that brings me peace. So I abandon my Planning, I abandon my Projections—I don't want those *P*s—and I head out the door.

Thinking, *Hell yeah. I feel awesome now.*

Question: Did any of my circumstances change? No. Is the likelihood that people won't accept me or love me or think what I have is good enough, was any of that any different from the five minutes before I headed out the door? No. It's not that I got myself to a place where I don't care what others think, or elevated above it. I returned home. I returned to reality. The only reality I want to live in: love, awesome.

Did I come up with some foolproof plan to safeguard me or my writing from rejection and scrutiny? No. And not just because it's not possible. But simply because I just didn't spend any energy on it.

This is a miracle. This is a freaking miracle. Can you imagine if the world operated this way?! And this isn't even the best part. Here's what happened next. Life! What a ride right?!

I got on a beautiful trail that I've never seen before. As I always do when I go for a walk or run, I tell my body to do what it needs. Run if you want. Walk if you want. You do you, boo.

And as I felt a little pep quicken in my step I took in the beauty around me. The cloudy morning, the small sliver of sun peeking through. I jogged across a bridge extending over a brook. I love a babbling brook! And shortly after that I saw the most adorable couple sitting under a tree.

Objectively it would be easy to miss what an adorable couple they were. They were middle-aged, they weren't dressed super-hip or in some conjured coordinated way. They were simply enjoying each other's company. His arm was lovingly wrapped around her as they chatted and took in the scenery. Their bikes were parked beside them as they sat side by side on a rock. They were centered under a beautiful golden tree losing its leaves to fall and framing them and their bikes perfectly. The black bikes in front of the yellow trees in front of the rolling southern Utah red rock were just too good.

I was so taken by the scene, I was so taken by their beauty, that I stopped jogging, without thinking, and said enthusiastically, "This is incredible! You two look incredible! Would you like me to take a picture?"

They were a tad startled but gave only a slightly hesitant yes! I could see that they wanted a picture, so I said, "It's no problem! I'd love to!" So they happily handed me their phone. I backed up a bit and I took off with it! Just kidding. I said, "I'm going to take a few, okay?"

Right as I was offering to take their picture two women on a walk passed by and said to me, "Oh my! Aren't you sweet! Make sure you capture their bikes. It's so cute!"

And I enthusiastically agreed. To both me being sweet and capturing the bikes.

I took the picture; they said thank you. And I jogged on. But as I left I started thinking that I had no idea what that moment was for them.

I had no idea if his arm was around her because they were in love and felt joy. Or if they were discussing something hard and he was offering support. I have no idea if it was an ordinary moment or a special day. All I know is that I was not so stuck inside myself I couldn't see the beauty in other people. I wasn't so anxious, I wasn't so wrapped up inside my feelings of fear or inadequacy or being an impostor and on and on.

Because I felt peace. Because I felt awesome, I was able to capture that moment for someone else. And as I captured that moment for someone else, another someone else (the walkers) witnessed it and felt that joy too.

How many times have I not seen the sweet couple under the tree? How many times have I not noticed the beautiful mountains that erupt on the horizon as I drive home every single day?

So many times.

Life is big! Life is complicated! Life is scary! And I'm not dismissing your pain and your problems and saying they are simple. They can't all be fixed with a jog.

There's inequality and injustice. There's deep, deep suffering. Not just for individuals but for nations. It all feels so much bigger than me. I feel so unqualified to speak to any of it. And then again . . . I used to feel really awful a lot of the time. And now, I do not.

I wake up and see the connectedness of the whole. By dealing with myself I get outside myself.

I felt so good after this whole experience, I stretched out my arms in my large long-sleeve shirt, like an airplane, and let the wind billow my shirt like sails as I strutted along the trail.

Three bikers sped by so fast I didn't have time to pretend I was an adult. This delighted them and the first one shouted, "Watch out! She's going to take off!" And then all three cyclists proceeded to mimic my airplane arms with glee.

I clearly heard the message: *The Universe! It's always figuring your problems out for you! Alison, feel awesome, put your damn arms out and if people want to put their arms out and feel awesome, too, they will.*

Put your arms out. Feel the wind. Surrender to the flow. Get ready to take off. Here we go!

1

I Can Wake Up to My Awesome!

To recognize one's own insanity is, of course,
the arising of sanity, the beginning of
healing and transcendence.

—ECKHART TOLLE

Ultimately, each of the eleven following shifts will invite you to come back to the core of this first one: *I can wake up to my awesome!* What we're doing currently isn't working. I'm not going to pretend to know your life. But I'm guessing if you grabbed this book, you're sick of analyzing if every decision you made was the right one. You're sick of beating yourself up for what you said or didn't say. For what you got done or didn't get done. You really want to stop feeling like everyone hates you or figure out a way to make lasting friendships or a love connection.

Maybe you're like me and you don't want to live with the skin-crawling torture of constant anxiety anymore. You're hoping to let go of self-harm or defeatist thoughts. Maybe you don't want any of these things, you just need more money, to lose weight, and get that dream job—because you think that will solve all those other problems. That's fine too! I can work with that.

But what we're doing, living this lie that our value is determined by what we create, or the value others give us, the lie that changing our circumstances will make everything better, isn't working.

This first shift is about choosing to awaken to a higher consciousness. To awaken to your awesome.

I'm not saying anything new; it's what every ancient spiritual tradition and the root of every religion have pointed to since the eons of time. What quantum physics and other studies of ecology and the Universe keep uncovering. The same message that Lao Tzu, Buddha, Jesus, and many others taught, dressed up in different words. It's the message I've already alluded to: you are not your form; you are consciousness, you are expansive. You are not the self; you are connected to the whole. As many different teachers have said in one way or another (and this is my favorite visual), you are not the cloud, you are the sky.

You might be turned off to spirituality, or what is referred to as woo-woo (which is insanely dismissive for something millions of people practice), because it doesn't use the same words as your religion, and this makes you uncomfortable or nervous.

Maybe all of it turns you off because people claiming to be

spiritual or religious have done really crappy things to you and continue to do crappy things. Maybe when I say God or Jesus there are too many constructs that trigger past wounds. I've been in a place where if people just said the word *God* I tuned out and dismissed them. Maybe religion excluded, condemned, or hurt you or ones you love. This happens so frequently. I honor and see you.

All these reasons and more are why I've pussyfooted around spirituality a lot in my teachings until now. I have a mixed relationship with religion, and at the end of the day I believe a lot of us can be religious without being spiritual. Alternatively a lot of us can claim spirituality and miss the whole point.

The point being? You can sit in the deep, wonderful place of knowing and peace inside you if you manage to not attach to your thoughts, your form. If you can, as Garth yells to Wayne as he's dreaming of buying a Fender Stratocaster, "Stop torturing yourself, man. . . . Live in the now!"

And so I'll use a lot of different terms and words to describe what "awesome" is. Universe, energy, nature, God, spirit, soul, and so forth. Some more than others. I'll reference lots of spiritual texts and teachings as well as pop songs, movies, and books. Because truth is everywhere! But at the end of the day, *awesome* will be a code word for these different terms and words, and you can follow what feels good and true for you.

This might drive some people crazy! And while I don't want to be frustrating, it also kind of delights me because I'm happier living in the questions than the answers. But I invite you to substitute words that resonate with your belief system, your soul, words, and concepts for "awesome" that light you up, and make you exhale in relief. When in doubt, follow the deep sighs of relief. In this book, in life, in conversations with a friend. Follow the relief, follow the joy.

I find so much joy knowing my divine worth. But you can get through this whole book and bypass the divinity part and still get a lot out of it. Your "awesome" is just my word for you recognizing you are more than form, a way to restore us to sanity. It is our higher consciousness, our awareness, the witness.

And in no way do you need to suddenly go from believing nothing, to something. A lot of what I share is based in and backed up by psychology and other hard sciences. But I believe that this understanding gives added depth and fun to combatting the lie that my value is determined by the value I create. The feeling of my intrinsic divine worth reinforces that my value is nonnegotiable. And that my worth is *not* determined by any subjective physical standard, but that my value is infinite, it is connected to the whole, and it is awesome.

So why choose to believe that you can "wake up to your awesome"? Because you get to choose what you do with your inner world no matter what. THAT IS FREEDOM! Believing that peace, joy, success, happiness, and well-being come from outside ourselves rather than from within simply isn't working for most of us.

Howard Thurman, civil rights leader and author, wrote, "Don't ask what the world needs. Ask what makes you come alive, and go do it. Because what the world needs is people who have come alive."

The shift of your focus and awareness to "I can wake up to my awesome!" reminds us to come alive. Reminds us to wake up. Not because you have some God-given right to feel "good." But because you *are* good. You *are* great. You *are* awesome. Stop falling asleep on yourself.

I Think Therefore I Am?

How can you choose to wake up to your awesome? By beginning to unlearn the lie that you are what you think. That you are your thoughts. That your thoughts and your perception are reality.

You can feel awesome now, literally right this second, by realizing that how you see the world, how you see that fight you just had with your mom, how you see the snotty comment someone just left you, how you see your body, is not reality. It's just how you're choosing to see it.

This sounds really, really heady, and it is, but I've also quoted *Wayne's World* in this chapter so don't feel like this is beyond comprehension. I'll say this a few different ways and then jump into easy application—so stick with me!

The introduction to the spiritual text *A Course in Miracles* teaches: Nothing real can be threatened. Nothing unreal exists. Herein lies the peace of God.[2]

In other words, love is real, God is real, your awesomeness and greatness are real. Peace! Peace is REAL. Everything else is perception.

That perception is of the world of form, thoughts, emotion, what Lao Tzu in the *Tao Te Ching* calls "the ten thousand things."[3]

One of the best books on the planet is Don Miguel Ruiz's *The Four Agreements*. In its introduction he writes a parable about a man who has a dream in which he realizes that everything is made of light.

"Everything in existence is a manifestation of the one living being we call God. Everything is God." And he came to the conclusion that human perception is merely light perceiving light. He also saw that matter is a mirror—everything is a mirror that reflects light and creates images of that light—and the world of illusion, the Dream, is just like the smoke that doesn't allow us to see what we really are. "The real us is pure love, pure light," he said.

At the end of the story when the man wakes up from his dream he doesn't want to forget all he has learned. So he decides to call himself the Smokey Mirror:

> I am the Smokey Mirror, because I am looking at myself in all of you, but we don't recognize each other because of the smoke in-between us. That smoke is the *Dream*, and the mirror is you, the dreamer.[4]

We are all looking at the world through our own smoky mirrors. The lie we believe is that the murky mirror is our reality. And how do we perceive this abstract reality? With our sneaky little thoughts. The meaning we create with them, the emotions that arise from them, and the actions that seem to just happen because of them.

Here's why I say sneaky!

We have anywhere from twelve thousand to sixty thousand thoughts per day. But according to some research, as many as 98 percent of them are exactly the same thoughts as we had the day before.[5] How? It does not feel that way, right?

Because you have conscious thought, and unconscious thought. This is why you don't have to consciously think about unzipping your pants every time you have to go to the bathroom. But also why you pick up your phone meaning to call your friend, and somehow find yourself on Facebook.

Even more significant, in my opinion, is that this same

research shows that 80 percent of our thoughts are negative. Those are some foggy, dirty, smoky mirrors.

My first instinct here was to learn how to manage and control all my thoughts. To reduce that 80 percent negative to something lower. Have you done this? Tried to control and judge all your thoughts and label them as bad or good? How's it working for you? How often do you find yourself falling into shame and despair because you can't seem to stop thinking about the thing you really didn't want to think?

"Come on, just think positive!"

"Don't be so negative."

"It's not that much blood, suck it up!"

More on beating yourself up later! But with all my mind control I realized I was trying to police the flow of life, my energy, my awesome, and everything else, and holy crap, it was exhausting. Don't think I wasn't committed! However, my thoughts were even more committed. THEY ARE STRONG! They are powerful, they are addictive. They are the ultimate drug.

Prevent the Spiral

Disarming the Power of Thoughts

I was having a conversation with a friend about an unpleasant confrontation she had with a neighbor. It was super uncomfortable for my friend, and of course, as is the way with neighbors, she would keep bumping into her. She wanted to know what to do. So I kept asking her what she felt. She said, "Well, it's crazy how she said . . ."

I asked again, "How do YOU feel?"

She answered, "My husband thinks that . . ."

"Hey, but how do YOU feel . . ." I said again.

And we went back and forth like this about ten times. I know, I'm such a fun friend! Finally I said, "Do you notice how many times I've asked how you felt?" She had not.

And she's not the only one who does this. We all do! Why is it so hard to get to the emotion that's stuck underneath so many situations? It's because of our thoughts about how we "should" feel, our thoughts about the other person. It's a whole lot of shame and blame and words words words. And none of them are reality. They are the smoky mirror.

I have the most wonderful group of humans I work with in an online paid community where I create new meditations and give a shift of focus each month. It's called Awesome on Demand, AOD for short. In a recent livestreaming session in which we were grappling with the concept "I am not my thoughts!," and that feeling our feelings is the only path to freeing ourselves from them, a member named Stephanie said:

"I think it's also very hard to say out loud how we feel. Like, I'm the teacher, the wife, the mother, and me, and I often feel like I'm just not enough but I don't like saying that out loud because I hate giving it life."

Ah! The shame. How many of us feel like Stephanie sometimes? Are you raising your hand too?! I told Stephanie that there is a lot of focus on positive thoughts and manifesting in the world of personal development right now, and those things are so great. But it can get tricky because we start to hide from our undesirable thoughts. We don't want to make them "real" or "manifest" them. But by shoving them down we are still giving them energy. They are still stuck in us! And they will keep popping up until they pass through us.

You are not your thoughts. You are not your emotions. Ignoring them will keep your focus on them, and keep you feeling like garbage. Waking up to the awareness that we are not these thoughts and feelings robs them of their power and disarms them of their hold on us.

Every single time we observe ourselves having a thought, we are waking up! We are waking up to our awesome, to our consciousness and awareness. How? By realizing, "I am not this thought!" or "I am not this emotion!" Instead "I am the awareness of it."

When we observe the thought, we can see where we're putting our focus, our sunshine, our light, our energy. And if we have made the commitment to feel awesome now, we can ask, "What is preventing me from peace? From feeling the awesomeness that I know is available to me?"

Here are three tools (of lots!) we can use to help wake us up to our awesome all day. Because what would be cool is if we can prevent the spiral into shame and blame, depression and anxiety, before it swallows us whole and we feel numb to it all. But even if that happens, that's okay too!

> **Notice your thoughts.** Attempt to witness them without labeling them as "good" or "bad." Just witness, "This is a thought." You can even follow up with, "I am not this thought!"

> **Notice how you avoid or want to squash certain thoughts.** Notice the feelings or emotions that arise

from those thoughts. Say, "I am not this emotion, I am awesome." This doesn't mean you're banishing it. It just means you distance yourself from it. Lean back! Relax, soften, and surrender.

Follow the trends! Stephanie's thought of *I am not enough* is a trend. She can be thinking about herself as a teacher, mother, wife, or person, and habitually end up at the same thought of *I am not enough.* Simply notice where you continually land. *Because our spirals, no matter how they start, tend to have the same destination.* They are simply habits. Observe the habit, and call it one. "I have this habit of ending up here, but it's not me, it's just a habit, habits can be changed." Don't worry about how yet! Just noticing it is HUGE! Just start to observe some of your common destinations. What's your Rome that all your thoughts seem to be leading to?

When in Doubt, TAP It Out

When feeling doubt, fear, insecurity, or anything else, you can always **TAP** it out to wake up to your awesome. Let's do it together.

TUNE IN: What are your thoughts, your feelings, your emotions? Give them a name, a color, a shape, or just a sound.

ACCEPT: Accept wholly and fully that you have this thought and feeling in this moment. You aren't this thought, but you're sure having it!

PICK YOUR FOCUS: Come into the present moment. Ask, *What is the moment teaching me? What is this moment asking of me so I can wake up to my awareness, my consciousness, my awesome?*

So shift number one: *awaken to your awesome.* No matter what you think about yourself, you are enough. You are not these thoughts. Life, the Universe, and your physical form will all take care of themselves, this is the true essence of awakening to your awesome. And you, my glorious friend, are freaking awesome.

2

I Don't Have to Figure Anything Out!

Don't worry so much about supposed to.

—LUC CLAIRMONT IN *CHOCOLAT*

The concepts of surrender and flow have always been so appealing to me. I want to surrender! I want to flow!

I'll be chill and easygoing and get a glorious tan as I cruise down the river of life. I just also want to make sure everybody loves me, no one is mad at me, and I get lots of stuff done. I'll flow, Universe!

Anyone else on my team?

That's why I was so excited to read Michael Singer's two books, *The Surrender Experiment* and *The Untethered Soul*. I loved them! This is how I used to tell people about them:

"Well, you should read *The Surrender Experiment* first because I was worried that if I surrendered I wouldn't be able to get all the big things done that I want to in life! But that book shows you that you can do both, surrender *and* be successful. So then when you read *The Untethered Soul* you can relax and really believe it and not worry it will make you complacent and not get you what you want!"

While I got a lot of the principles in the books, and they are completely life changing and helped me understand my "awesome" on a whole new level, it's hysterical to me that I missed the point. The point being that if I surrender, if I have an "untethered soul" I won't feel the need to base my worth on how much I accomplish, and how much value I create.

It's that damn lie again! The lie that I am not valuable unless I create value, unless other people give me value, it runs so deep in me it blinds me. It runs so deeply in us that we spend our lives figuring out how to create, earn, and keep this value, instead of realizing we already have it!

So much of my suffering has been born of my need to control, or I should say, my illusion of control. The need for control keeps us separated in fear from our truest selves, the selves that emerge when we accept and allow. We believe that with our thoughts and actions we can control the world around us and make it so things don't hurt us. Make the world fit, as Buddhism calls it, our preferences. Our likes and dislikes.

We note our preferences based on past experience or even just perceptions, and store them in ourselves, so we can try to figure out how to avoid the yucky, scary things and have more of the good things. So we can keep ourselves safe, so we can enjoy life, so we can bypass suffering and pain.

But is it actually working? Kind of? Sometimes? Occasionally, right?

We have decided what can and cannot happen in order for

us to feel how we want to feel. "I cannot lose them, I cannot be treated this way . . ." But it does not stop the world and other people from doing what they do. Yet we continue to imagine ourselves as master gamemakers! Who can arrange all the players and pieces in a way that will set us up for success. If we just figure it all out! Figuring things out is a euphemism for control.

But when we allow ourselves to have faith that the Universe, energy, or God will take care of itself, when we release and surrender, when we tap into that flow, the flow of divine universal timing, what happens? It moves us from being a piece in the game we are trying to control, to being a cocreator with the Universe. We're able to see more solutions, take clear inspired action, and feel less frantic. When we shift our focus to our expanded, connected consciousness, we don't lose power, we gain it.

Ask yourself if this has ever been true for you. When you get some space or "get out of your head," are you able to see things in a "new light"? See solutions that weren't there before or that you actually already had the thing you needed? This is one of the many reasons gratitude is so powerful! It helps you focus on what you do have instead of what you lack.

And how many times have you waited, not avoided but waited, and whatever you were trying to "figure out" took care of itself? This is an example of the principle called nonaction. Or in the forty-eighth verse of the *Tao Te Ching* as Lao Tzu says, "When nothing is done, nothing is left undone."

One of the many, many reasons we don't feel awesome, and we keep getting pulled out of the present moment and into our thoughts, is because we are spending our limited time, energy, and resources trying to figure something out.

Where Was the Money, Matt?!

My wonderful husband, Eric, and I both run our own individual businesses. He is a music producer and composer and has an online music library. But of course it didn't start that way. I worked full time until I had our first baby, and then I had the luxury of working a little freelance, and beginning to build my platforms and product ideas in the cracks of time early motherhood provides. Nap times, weekends, and of course bedtime until 2 a.m. or 3 a.m. Eric kept his day job, doing his music any time he could.

I had been experimenting with selling products at craft fairs, and selling digital patterns and designs. I was contributing to bigger blogs for some tiny paychecks, fifty dollars here and there, but I had no idea what any sort of business model would look like. I was just keeping busy, and having fun too. There was no pressure yet, no pressure to figure anything out.

When I was halfway through my pregnancy with our second child, a competing company with Eric's employer got a billion-dollar deal. They started hiring key players at Eric's company, which resulted in them needing to dramatically downsize Eric's department.

A few weeks before Christmas in 2012, my sweet husband came home to his pregnant wife and two-year-old and said, "Well, I lost my job today." He said it with a half smile, and a shrug, but also a deep sadness.

He walked over to me in our always messy kitchen, in our always messy house, and I uncharacteristically said nothing, as we just held each other for a very long time. I remember the olive-green maternity shirt I was wearing, and just wanting to hold Eric longer, absorbing his sadness. I was perfectly present. I felt peaceful, I felt calm. I felt heartbroken for him, but also happy because his job had been too good to leave and was keeping him from his true calling of music.

In that moment, I truly felt like there was nothing to figure out. And the steps forward readily appeared. After a few minutes I said, "Okay, I will make more money, and you will do your music. And it's going to be fine. I've always said I'm pretty sure I could make a million dollars, so I'll just do that, okay?" Eric was reluctant. He could get another job; he could go to the competing company. But I knew, my calm inner knowing was right, he needed to get started on bringing his sweet beats to the world.

So we sold a car, we lost our insurance, we had our second baby with government assistance. I made clothes for the little boy in my belly and somehow made just enough money to pay our bills selling handcrafted leather baby mobiles and contributing to other blogging sites with my writing. Eric started to build his music business and was able to get some contracts too.

We brought our baby boy home to a chaotic house full of instruments, recording equipment, craft supplies, party decor, and insanity.

Without thinking, without a set plan, the next five years flowed in terms of income. There were really tight months, but I just kept believing: *I have everything I need for this exact moment.*

Many months we'd have no clue how we were going to pay our bills next month. I always believed that an opportunity or idea would reveal itself. And it always did. We kept our expenses as low as possible, not taking big vacations or trying to buy a nicer living space, furniture, or cars.

I read some books about money and uncovered the insight that I had a limiting belief; that is, that it was selfish to make money. I shifted my mindset and kept building my business. Sometimes I made more, sometimes I made less. I always had exactly what I needed.

If you have limiting beliefs around money, apply every single shift in this book toward them. Tune in and accept and uncover what they are. It will take practice but you can heal them. There's nothing to figure out, just an opportunity to expand into your limitless self.

This all worked well and fine until about 2017, when I started making money mean something about my value. As I expanded my Build an Awesome Brand workshop, trained and hired brand coaches, and attracted other businesses to my workshops, I put more and more pressure on myself to make more money. *If you don't hit one million in sales this year, why should people listen to you, Alison?*

Never mind that I had everything I needed. Never mind that we were clothed and fed. *If I make more money, I can do more good!* Which is true, but if I needed more money to do more good at that moment, I would have made more money!

It was a problem I created. Simple as that. I had hired more team members, and wanted to pay them more, and wanted them to have faith in me. I needed everyone to know just how successful and legitimate I was. Meaning, I needed to prove it to myself. I forgot I was already as awesome as I need to be. And that's okay.

I was trying to figure something out that didn't need figuring! I had never promised people how to make more money at my workshop, but instead how to build businesses they loved, and how doing that does make you more money! IT DOES. I was trying to figure out how to make more money even though it had nothing to do with teaching people how to do what they feel called to do, and do it in a way that doesn't make them miserable.

In 2019 I spent half the year feeling like a failure, like I was washed up, like I couldn't expand and make money to save my life. Every month my profit and loss statements were dismal. Making more money to feed my machine became a constant issue I needed to figure out immediately. We'd spend hours and hours at work trying to organize, push, and force the expansion. Chart after chart, projection after projection.

And I was miserable. I believed I didn't deserve to teach anyone or speak anywhere unless I hit my target profit. I thought it was my actual job to "figure it out!" Of course lots of other forces were at play here. But I ignored all of them and made this one problem, making more money, trump all the other uncomfortable realities that needed healing and attention.

In the late summer of 2019 I decided to surrender. To stop trying to figure it out. Either I'd run it all into the ground or it would work out. I stopped making the profits of my business mean anything about me as a person. I started making clearer decisions and tending to underlying issues. I remember praying and saying, "I submit. I will no longer push my agenda, Thy will be done."

I didn't magically make more money. But I started seeing solutions. People were sent to me, the true underlying needs of my business started to surface.

In December we went to meet with our accountant, Matt, to prepare our taxes. I was shocked to learn my business had overall made more money than any year before. True, I was spending more money, but the business was still very profitable.

"Why did every month feel like such a struggle?! Why did I hardly ever have any money in my accounts? Why did I spend the year feeling like trash?" I said with dramatic flair. "WHERE WAS THE MONEY, MATT?!"

"Yeah, that sounds like a cash flow problem, supercommon," Matt said kindly.

"ARE YOU FREAKING KIDDING ME? You mean that thing I see on commercials, 'cash flow problem,' that's what this is? I make my money sporadically in bursts but my bills come regularly. I wasn't a failure all along?!"

Why didn't I talk to anyone about my anxieties around my business and money during this time? Because I was hiding from them, of course! Why didn't I see the solutions, options, and possibilities that had been there all along, people on my team willing to help me understand all that confusing money nonsense?! Because I was sucked into the fire of my problem, I couldn't stop staring at the flames. I was in the small mind of the yapping dog, making money mean something about my value as a human.

I had made it through six blissful years of business not needing to figure money out, allowing myself to flow, until I started to make it all mean something about me. Once it meant something about me, my value, my worth, as soon as it didn't feel like it was growing fast or big enough, I started needing to FIGURE IT OUT! But all I was doing was trying to control. I had everything I needed all along, but trying to figure it out became my top priority, so I could control my own perception of self. And it sucked all the joy from my soul!

Inspired Action Versus Frantic Action

So much of the feeling or the desire to "figure things out," no matter *what* the thing is, comes from a place I refer to as "frantic action."

The principle of inspired action over frantic action has changed my life. I've defined it for myself, but it might look and feel different for you. It's all good! Just follow what feels good! But here's how I personally live this law.

For me, frantic action is action for the sake of doing something. Frantic action is fueled by wanting to control or figure something out, a sense of lack or urgency that I'll be missing out, or fear. Frantic action always asks me to keep moving, says that my feelings are not valid, and affirms I am worthless if I stop moving and producing.

I realized that much of the action I used to take was frantic action. And it's not because I meant to, or that I'm just so neurotic and unique. I took action this way because I'm a human living right now. Most of us are taking frantic action and believe it is the *only* way to operate.

Why? I believe it's because most of us are operating with dysregulated nervous systems. Yes, our actual physical bodies are freaking out! Our nervous systems, which are foundational in so much of what we perceive and feel, cannot figure out which threat is *real* or which is only *perceived*. It is due to both recent and past trauma, ancestral and personal, and the bananas reality of living in our overstimulating social-media-run society. Not to mention we are at a whole new breaking point after the collective year of worldwide trauma in 2020 and beyond.

Much of the world's frantic action stems from the much-talked-about response of the sympathetic nervous system: fight or flight. When presented with a stressor, which can be as tiny as feeling threatened for one second, the fight-or-flight response can flood our body with chemicals and reflexes for safety and protection. Frantic action screams in every cell of your body, "Step up NOW, ready or not, and fight!" Or "RUN! There is danger here, flee!"

This isn't easy to just change overnight. It's wired in our body's cells. But noticing and being aware of this frantic action in yourself is like the single match that can set a forest ablaze. So don't give up yet!

Another tricky thing about frantic action is that it totally abides by Newton's first law of motion: an object at rest stays at rest and an object in motion stays in motion with the same speed and in the same direction unless acted upon by an un-balanced force.

Let's be clear, I absolutely used to unconsciously believe my value as a human directly correlated to the work I created. I tied my worth nearly 100 percent to the goals I achieved. I believed if I did better, bigger work, I would feel less anxious and more people would approve of me. HA! But, when I hit my goals, I felt more deserving and valuable. This made me feel safe, for a moment. But believing that I would stop hitting goals, and dis-appoint everyone, myself included, caused me to take frantic ac-tion from a place of fight, flight, and fear for over three decades. The "cash flow issues" that had me feeling worthless were new; the need to prove my worth was not.

Like Newton said, we are objects in motion or at rest. And unless a very strong outside, unbalanced force acts on us, we will all keep swimming like a shark, swimming for our lives (fight) or sink into hours and hours of scrolling social media or watching television and numbing (flight). We stay in the motion we are in until a new force appears.

So what force am I suggesting to knock your world off-kilter? INSPIRATION. Yes! Inspired action, as taught through the Law of Attraction, is action that moves with faith, action that has vision and perception. Action that knows its pace is perfect! This inspired action, that I interchangeably refer to as flow, brings balance and peace to our weary minds. And it brings peace and balance to this weary, rest-starved world.

Inspired action asks us to replace force with flow. It invites us to change the direction we are headed. Inspired action is the catalyst that knocks us into needed rest or joyful motion. How does it choose? The inspired choice and subsequent action or nonaction will always affirm light and life! How can you know if you are taking inspired action? Is it affirming your light and life? Or diminishing it? Frantic action is fueled by fear, and fear aims to diminish.

Inspired action requires we trade fear for faith, and not keep mindlessly yanking on life like it's a slot machine we have to nurse and control. When we stop treating life like some rigged cashbox with lights, when we stop believing the only game to play is one that runs us ragged with figuring out. When we stop playing the same slots over and over, and walk away from the game of frantic action that has done nothing but distract and drain us, we can finally realize in so many ways, we've already hit the jackpot.

My process for taking inspired action in my own life is best summed up by one of my favorite quotes, "Arrange whatever pieces come your way" (Virginia Woolf).

There is so much beauty and instruction here.

When we try to figure things out, we take frantic action

mostly based on what we believe will give us a certain result. We're usually miserable and worried taking the action, and then miserable and worried if it doesn't work out, and then miserable and worried if it does work out, because then we have to figure out how to always keep it the way we want it. How to keep the boyfriend, the money, the good job, the naughty body.

When we take inspired action, we arrange the pieces we have. This requires gratitude. Gratitude doesn't happen in the past or the future. That's the power of gratitude, its presence. When we use gratitude to see what "pieces" we already have, solutions and pathways present themselves.

Inspired action requires "arranging." Arranging is an art, not a science. All of us will create different, unique bouquets with the pieces we are given. There's no wrong! How awesome is that?

The small phrase "come your way" invites faith, hope, and vision for a world and reality that is beyond your limited perspective.

Inspired action speaks in the language of love, and frantic action speaks in the language of shame and fear.

Swap Your Frantic Figuring for Inspired Flow, and You'll Go, Baby, Go!

To me, goals are overrated. Think how much time you've spent trying to "figure out" something specifically as it pertains to a "goal" you have.

Even a really nice goal, like "Spend more time with family," is often a bully in disguise. A bully who taunts and plants doubt and asks you to prove how worthy and valuable you are by living up to it. The action in service of this goal feeds a false reality. The action isn't a bully all by itself; spending time with family can be great, but the reason that propels the action—it's usually a jerk. In this case you might want to spend more time with family because you've decided that even though they cross your boundaries repeatedly, you want to be a good person. And a good person spends time with family. This goal is a bully because it stems from a reality where you must constantly combat and prove your worth. In truth, action that brings understanding and joy always comes from a place of flow, not force.

Goals are the product of a patriarchal society that places a heavy emphasis on DOING MORE. Don't waste energy fussing with those silly, impermanent feelings that can't even be understood! Goals can be. So goals can be sold as facts. Goals are measurable. Hence, we love goals. And yet in return for all our love and obedience to them, goals often become a suppressor of self. Maybe good intentions pave the path to hell, but fixating on self-worth-affirming goals creates hell on earth.

So how do you practice or invite flow?

You trade goals for intentions centered in your inherent worth. Then, when you add in a sincere practice of having faith that you are already awesome, this will always result in flow. You invite flow when you practice faith in the value of your worth and goodness, faith that you do not need to prove your individual or collective worth, and faith that YOU DO NOT NEED TO FIGURE ANYTHING OUT or crush some goal to be awesome. You are already awesome and so is the action that will flow from your unique strengths and talents. Not trying to control what you share and say, not trying to figure it all out, is allowing flow.

Working in flow allows you to share your gifts with more ease and lightness. Living in flow will improve your physical, emotional, mental, and spiritual health. Living in flow has changed me for the lighter. Releasing all the "figuring out" of the mind and allowing the flow of your spirit will heal you, and in turn heal the world.

Each of these shifts is meant to wake you up, prevent a spiral, and invite you to shift your awareness to invite awesomeness in. I want you to say them out loud, to question them, to ask, "How would believing this make me feel?"

This will help you feel the love, light, and peace that is begging for your attention. How does believing you don't have to figure anything out do that? When you stop trying to figure life out, life starts flowing through you. Where your energy flows grows! Like water, you will feel more and more limitless. It's so beautiful!

For a moment let's think about the way water moves and behaves. It's hard when it needs to be, soft when it needs to be; it's both gentle and powerful. It moves decisively, never questioning, never halting. It's not figuring, it's flowing.

It seems effortless in its movement because of the beautiful dancelike way it undulates and turns. Water is so sexy! A river surges from one powerful source, and like a river our actions and movements can also surge from our most powerful source, if we let them! That source being love, light, awareness, yes, our awesome. When we decide to not use thought to figure all the things out, but instead lean into flow, that's what we're signing up for: seemingly effortless inspired action! It's freaking fantastic, it's ecstasy, I kid you not.

If you personally don't have to figure anything or everything out, it raises a really good question: What or who then will take care of life?

But as a thought exercise, what if life takes care of and figures itself out? What if the tree knows the exact moment to surrender its leaf, and the bird the exact moment to leave its nest? And in that same way you can flow from action to action, with a quiet knowing, a steady inner guide?

What if instead of more figuring, we did more flowing?

Prevent the Spiral

Invite Inspiration Daily; It's Looking for You!

My favorite tools for taking inspired action all involve quick but quiet moments to invite its catalyst: inspiration. If you don't invite inspiration to the party, she is a lot less likely to show up, so give her a holler daily! Here are my steps for inviting inspiration into your life.

Slow down. Often in conversations, during keynotes, or even when ordering food, I'll notice my energy start to get fast and excited and a bit frantic. Slowing everything down allows for flow to pour in and to take momentum away from frantic. Like how water can break down a rock. Sometimes I just stop and take a breath midsentence. I TAP to feel awesome now. Sometimes I just slow down to sense the other person's or the room's energy. Of course meditation is an insanely helpful tool for taking inspired action. The silence tells us more than words ever could.

Pay close attention to the process. Rather than allowing the results, like someone's reaction or the success of a business decision, to mean anything, I look at the process. Inspired action feels good. It often feels easy and effortless. This might freak your brain out because we've spent so much time believing the lie that we need to suffer and toil to create value. When I help train my team to work in flow they often say, "I don't feel like I'm doing any work! I need to work more!" I felt that way at first too. But you'll start to realize you're getting way more done in way less time.

Effort, yes. Force, no. Work, yes. Shame, no. Inspired action invites you to allow, not push. Allow the expansion; you don't have to figure it out and force it.

Acting on inspiration and the process of flow IS the result, regardless of what happens next.

Look outside your usual markers of success. When we act on inspiration and then things don't go like we expected (usually meaning they don't go well), we start to doubt that we were inspired at all. But that's not true! So to save myself from the doubt spiral and find a way to keep carrying on in the flow, I look to new places I didn't used to look for markers of success.

My markers of success are now, "Was the action motivated by love, light, or inspiration?" Yes?! Okay, good.

"Did I feel joy, ease, or like I was guided during the process?" Yes? CRUSHING IT!

"Did I remember to focus on the one?" Especially in my work it's so easy to get lost in the scale of it. How many followers, how many downloads, how many sales. But love is shared from one heart to one heart. And I believe inspired action leads me to the one. I look for the one. The one person who says, "I really, really needed that." Or often the one is me. Maybe I was the one who needed it, needed to learn the lesson, or try that path that went nowhere. I believe in the one.

Just Open Your Arms

Right before the world shut down in 2020 my husband and I were lucky enough to go to Cancun. We decided to do a tree-top zip line tour. I hadn't zip-lined in WHO knows how long! So when Hugo (our awesome tour guide) quickly hooked me in—gave me basically zero instruction, then thrust me up as the sacrificial lamb to go first—I momentarily panicked. "Are you ready?!" Hugo asked. "Wait! Am I supposed to do anything?!" I gasped frantically right as he was about to let go.

He smiled the BEST smile, and said, "Just open your arms!" His incredible choice of words THRILLED ME. I just opened my arms and squealed like a giddy six-year-old careening through the treetops of the Mayan jungle. It was so freaking beautiful. And I enjoyed every second of it!

"Just open your arms" is the antidote to trying to figure things out. Just open your arms and feel awesome. Bless Hugo for the wording! He reminded me to surrender to the moment, be open to receiving the good, the uncomfortable, the pleasurable, the unknown.

All the good stuff comes in the surrender. In not needing to control, or hustle or push or coerce. I swear. Trust me. Or trust Hugo. Just open your arms. It's all going to work out, and really the only task is to do what you can to enjoy the ride.

3

I Can Choose
My Freaking Focus!

When you understand, you cannot help but love.

—THICH NHAT HANH

My nephew James is one of the most wonderfully grumpy four-year-olds. He often greets you by just saying, "NO!" Or "I don't want to!" He kind of growls when he says most things, and if you put him in a pair of New Balance sneakers and Dockers, he's the happiest kid on the block. He will tolerate only one friend, but also loves just puttering around the house doing his own thing. He's a lot like a ninety-year-old man. He's my sister's little guy, and my sister, Andrea, and I are close, so I hear all about James and his adventures regularly. The other morning Andrea asked how James slept and he said, "Oh, I had a really scary nightmare." Very matter-of-factly. So Andrea said, "Oh, I'm so sorry! What was it about?" And James reported, "There were three skeletons chasing me and they were trying to bash my head in and then I woke up." Andrea asked if James was able to fall back asleep after such a scary dream and he said, "Oh, yeah. Mom, you know how your brain is kind of like a television screen? I just changed the channel. I changed the channel so I could fall back asleep."

It's no wonder James is so grumpy! He's an enlightened little soul, and he doesn't have time to waste with all the nonsense the world is trying to thrust upon him! But James's description of switching the channel (which, incidentally, is a very common and widely taught principle when it comes to consciousness) is my favorite example of the shift *I can choose my freaking focus!* The basis of the concept is so simple, even a four-year-old can comprehend it. We get to, in each moment, every day, and for the rest of our life, choose what to focus our attention on.

As always, just because this is simple, it doesn't mean it's easy to do!

I remember crying under a desk at Hallmark Inc. during my internship there in 2006. The wildly successful greeting card company built its foundation on creativity and housed (and probably still does) the most beautiful library for its creative team. I was under my desk hyperventilating, as one does when one is me, having a very scary panic attack. I knew I needed to do something before someone found me under there, so I got myself to the library and started looking for a book to help.

I found a book called *Zen and the Art of Motorcycle Maintenance*. Zen sounded like something I needed so I sat on the floor of the library and started to read through my tears.

The introduction talks about how little awareness we have of our mind and our thoughts and asks us to imagine if we had the same amount of control over our body as we do our mind.

The example shared was that you wouldn't be able to focus your body long enough to safely cross a street.

That was one of the first times I realized how little awareness I had of my thoughts and where they took me. And that it might possibly be a lack of this awareness, which at the time I automatically decided was a lack of control, that had brought me to sitting helplessly under my desk, at an internship where I very much wanted to impress rather than concern people.

You Are Not a Robot, You Are a Warrior

The decision to feel awesome is the decision to return to your awareness, to your consciousness and your highest self. It's a practice, a practice of letting go of the lies of form—that your value is outside of you—and returning to the truth of who you are. And this decision will ask a lot of you; it will ask you to uncover what, even in the most difficult of circumstances, you want to freaking focus on. What you want to turn the screen of your mind to.

It will ask you to believe, "I get to choose my experience of this event moving forward. What do I want that experience to be?"

Each moment asks: What do you want to flip the channel to right now? What do you want to see? Not what do you want to ignore or repress! On the contrary, redirecting our focus back to consciousness, back to awareness, back to awesome, keeps us living in the present.

Let's go back to me hyperventilating under my desk. First let's just establish: it's perfectly fine to hyperventilate under your desk. It's perfectly fine to freak out, and not be able to consciously choose your freaking focus and have a panic attack. I will have more panic attacks and outbursts. I had an outburst last night with my children for not staying in their freaking beds. "WHY DO I HAVE TO YELL FOR YOU TO LISTEN TO ME?!!" I screamed at their tiny frightened faces, shaking with anger.

Deciding to feel awesome is not about becoming a robot who handles every situation flawlessly. Doing everything perfectly does not result in a perfect life. *Perfect* is another messy, loaded word, *perfect* is a construct. I'm a perfect mother if I decide that perfect mothers occasionally scream, but later apologize. Which I did. See, I'm perfect. WHAT A RELIEF!

Making the shift of allowing yourself to choose your focus is not about being perfect and never choosing wrong. Instead, it powerfully reminds us that no matter what, we get to be creators of our life. And because you choose to continue creating, even after others have hurt you, even after you've decided it's too difficult, because you keep showing up—doesn't matter if it's in the fetal position or on horseback—YOU ARE A WARRIOR.

The places where our energy and focus flow, grow. We get to decide what we want to nurture, what experiences we want to create in each new moment. Focus is one of the most powerful tools of creation we have.

You are not some hapless bystander. You can wake up to your awesome, choose your freaking focus, find a path to peace, and do the damn thing. Whatever the damn thing of the day is! Or you can get back under the desk and take the time you need. Whichever it is, choose it! And choose what is truth for you; both are acts of love and courage when they are your truth.

Every time you remember to choose your focus, reward

yourself! This is different from controlling your focus. A choice often requires an act of creation. It requires listening and realizing there are options. So when you celebrate the times you're able to choose your focus, rather than have it dictated, you'll create a positive feedback loop. Choose to focus on the fact that you woke up to your awesome! You realized you'd lost sight of your inherent awesomeness, but you've noticed it, and chose to come back to it. VICTORY! Celebrate your triumphant return prodigal son style! It's okay you lost the family fortune; we're just glad to have you back.

Even if the awareness comes after choosing or losing your focus in a way that you're ashamed of, you still deserve to find your focus again. After yelling at my kids I felt horrible. But instead of choosing to focus on my mistake, which had passed, I focused on the present moment. In the present moment I felt a deep sadness for my three cute kids. They were being so annoying but they're also really cute and kind. They often listen without me screaming. So in the present moment I chose to forgive myself for my outburst so I could focus on their cuteness, on their soft hearts being hurt by a tired, frustrated mother, and I went back downstairs to apologize.

When in Doubt, TAP It Out!

Choosing a freaking focus is different from just choosing any old focus. I could have chosen to focus on the fact I've no doubt scarred my children, but that doesn't guide me toward joy, or solutions. In the case of my outburst at my children, I chose to appreciate a chance to model a truth for them and return to truth myself. The truth that we can all make mistakes and apologize. It's hard for it to feel true sometimes, that we are worthy of forgiveness, but if we can't believe it for ourselves, we can't believe it for others.

The first step of choosing your focus is simply noticing and being aware that you have one. You do, even if it's buried deep. Once it surfaces, or even if it won't, I then like to ask if what I'm focusing on stems from love or fear? Is my focus rooted in a sense of abundance or lack?

The TAP it out method I've introduced is the next step after being aware you have a focus, and it will help you to pick a new or truer focus that will guide you back to your intention to feel the awesome that already courses through you.

Let me walk you through the TAP method using the scenario we just discussed. If I had been able to TAP it out when I was hyperventilating under my desk at my internship, here's what I could have done.

TUNE IN: How was I feeling? Heartbroken, confused, overwhelmed. My partner of five years and I were breaking up. The entire world I thought I had known was ending. It hurt. I was feeling hurt, but probably more a loss of control. How do I know? Because that's the thing that usually gets me under a desk in despair. The loss of control. It stirs up unfathomable fear, and so I hide.

And even though it feels unfathomable, this fear so many of us know, you can trust that your spirit and body seek to balance your ability to stay conscious. Try not to fight against it, and your body can feel the pain, sadness, or hurt you don't think you can. You CAN feel it, know that pain, and be alive. It doesn't always feel true. I know it doesn't. I really, really know it doesn't. But you can know the hard, and the bad, and the gross and still focus on your strength instead. You are a warrior. You can see and know your pain and survive. I believe in you.

I didn't believe I could witness the immense and complicated pain a horribly abusive relationship, and its torturous breakup, created. So I didn't acknowledge the pain was there. I didn't know there was another option other than forcing myself forward. Hence my panic attack under a desk.

In retrospect, if I had tuned in, I might have been able to see some pain and I could have called in sick. But I know me, and I know I would not have allowed it. I didn't know I could do what I needed for me, which would have been keening in my bed and allowing the heartbreak and suffering to sit in my body and course through me like waves. I didn't know I had a choice.

So I forced myself to go to work and not feel what I was feeling, because I didn't know how.

"But Alison!" you might object. "You needed to go to work!"

Did I? Was it better that I went to work and had a panic attack under my desk? Was that internship more important than my emotional well-being? My focus was on holding it together. I'm not saying we become ruled by our emotions, I'm saying that we're already ruled by our emotions and thoughts, because we keep thinking they can hold all the power or none. We hide from them, or blindly follow them, not realizing they're pulling the strings. Rather than witnessing them from our place of awesome, our soul, our highest self, we think we are our thoughts and feelings. And then we feel even more terrible.

And who's to say that if I had tuned in, and journaled and felt and sobbed, rather than pushing the feelings away, that I wouldn't have been able to make it through a day at work? I'm a warrior and you are too. Let's not underestimate ourselves.

Let's keep going on this path of choosing to TAP it out.

ACCEPT: I could have accepted that I was heartbroken. That I thought I was going to marry him and be with him forever and that not being able to control that was really, really uncomfortable—to say the least. If I had made the decision to choose my focus, I could have explored why this circumstance disturbed me so much. Not just that it hurt me, because of course it did! Ending a relationship is painful! But why was it resulting in panic attacks? With acceptance comes curiosity and compassion. Compassion I desperately needed. Also, with acceptance comes less anxiety, just saying.

I might have also accepted that I was unable to feel awesome on my own and that it was time to seek help. I might have been able to see that therapy, counseling, or some other sort of new spiritual practice was needed. I needed help. I so badly needed help. I did not know I needed it, or how to go about getting it.

I am not, and will not, beat myself up for my past. I was doing the best I could with the understanding that I had. Whatever experience this story is bringing up for you in your own life: you are doing the best you can. You did the best you could. My best looked like me continuing this pattern of anxiety and breakdowns and the denial of my pain for another decade. And thank Goddess! Thank the Universe it did because that's what I needed to learn that living that way does not work. I tried, I swear it does not work—not noticing your pain or hurt. It always surfaces. And now that I know I am a warrior and not a robot, I don't care how freaking uncomfortable this decision to FEEL AWESOME makes me. Yes, it is difficult letting go of my ego and false sense of identity and safety; at some points it has felt like I'm walking through hell. And it's STILL better than my life full of anxiety and fear.

Choosing to accept my feelings, and feel them even when they are awful, is bringing me to joy, to expansion, to true freedom. And what is true freedom? To be able to move through this world, knowing you cannot control it, and yet no matter what happens, knowing you will be okay. That you can choose your focus, and with each experience, you can peel back yet another layer of the incredible warrior of light and truth that you are.

What guided me to the library? That light. That intuition, my awesome. It was always there, it will always be there, and I can bask in it, return to it, and live in it more and more when I choose the focus of feeling as awesome as I am.

Think back to something like this in your life. A crying-under-the-desk moment. What got you from there to this book? Because you're here, right? You made it through.

"But, Alison, I don't want to ever go through that again, please, please, I beg you, don't make me do it again."

I hear you. That's not what we're focusing on. What got you from there to here? The core of you that reaches for light, the consciousness of you that says, *I can keep going, I will keep going.* Whether it was something that depletes and drains you, like a belief that you'd be selfish to quit, or something that fuels you, like maybe the thought *I can do hard things!* You're here. You did it.

But the force, the pushing, the coercion, the hustle? Ignoring your physical, mental, and emotional limits? It cannot take you where you want to go. It might have gotten you here and we honor and thank it for that. But if you want peace, if you want your load lightened, if you want to take inspired action and not be riddled with confusion and fear, it can't be the gas that fuels you anymore.

PICK YOUR FOCUS: Focus on the present. What did I have in that moment? The perfect experience to guide me to a greater understanding. Knowing this wouldn't have magically taken away the pain. But it would have allowed the pain to pass through me sooner. I carried pain from the relationship for years and years. The actual breakup dragged on for another year even after this event. Truly, only time and distance finally helped me see what a horrific situation I had survived. The one I pushed away while it was happening because I couldn't see it for what it was at the time. I was stuck in pain. In panic, in fear.

And that's what trauma does. It literally gets stuck in our brain. And we can't seem to get it out. Flashbacks, reliving past conversations over and over. It robs us of the present. When we choose to feel awesome now, when we use the shift of *I can choose my freaking focus!*, we take back our power to navigate our pain, see more clearly, and turn the television of our mind to a channel that brings us healing and peace.

What I had at that present moment was a huge library full of books and resources. I had a place to cry and the perfect teacher showing up in my life for greater empathy that would fuel my life mission.

You can do this now. You can go back to an experience that has wounded you. And please do it with the aid of a trauma therapist or spiritual guide, coach, or counselor if needed. And create a new experience or understanding of it.

Bring your highest, most loving awesome self, to the version of you hyperventilating under the desk, and see if you can't help her TAP it out.

You can ask what pain got stuck in there, and see if it's ready to be felt. It might not be, and that's okay too. You'll have the awareness that it's there and it can now stop robbing you of future peace and stop dictating how you show up in the world.

We All Have a Driving Question; Where's Yours Taking You?

As important and powerful as the shift of *I can choose my freaking focus!* is for any given moment, or any isolated incident, it's even more important and powerful when put in the context of your life.

Your focus is a driving question, whether you realize it or not.

In early 2014 I started a series on YouTube called *How to Be Awesome.* Now to put this in perspective, I had already been blogging, selling handmade goods, and sharing online for over seven years at this point.

As an introduction to the series, I wrote:

> Hey! So I've wanted to do this video series for a while! It's called *How to Be Awesome.*
>
> Not because I think I'm awesome; as I've mentioned before I operate on like a 50/50 basis. Fifty percent of the time I think I'm awesome and 50 percent of the time I think I'm, like, worthless. So yeah, I wanted to start this series not because I think I'm awesome, but because I thought it would be nice to have a place to talk about what to do when you're not feeling awesome. And ways to extract even more awesomeness from yourself.

In this same year, and because they liked the *How to Be Awesome* YouTube series, Microsoft hired me to host a slew of events for influencers all over the country for their search engine Bing. I called it the Search for Your Awesome tour. I know. I'm a freaking events genius. But a freaking genius who was driven by one unrelenting, unforgiving, and fairly ruthless question.

The question that led to the creation of so much good—events, relationships, products, and self-discovery—was the same question causing me to feel worthless much more than 50 percent of the time. The same question that later that year was the cause of months after months, and most likely a lifetime, of anxiety attacks. It is a question that seems well-intentioned, sincere, and masquerades itself as altruistic and noble. My driving question for almost my entire life:

HOW CAN I BE MORE AWESOME?

My heart physically hurts to look at 2014 Alison, who was doing her absolute best, at all times, to figure out how to BE more awesome.

Because what's the real underlying question there?

HOW CAN I BE MORE?

The questions we ask hold more answers about ourselves than any response possibly could. They reveal our focus, and where we are looking for value.

What a question like this reveals is that I really believed I wasn't enough. And in order to be enough, enough of whatever it is I wanted to be, I had to DO more. I had to search for more. I had to BE more awesome.

More people had to approve of me, more people needed to know and praise me, and my accomplishments had to fill up the unattainable and always leaky bucket of MORE.

I now understand that I believed my power needed to be claimed externally. I had to be the future, better, more awesome version of Alison NOW. Which meant I rarely lived in the present, and frantically tried to control the future.

Maybe as a chubby ten-year-old I had all but given up trying to claim that power with my body. No one approved of that from early on; it was too big, too loud, and simply too much. Which is maybe why for the rest of my life I've felt I had to work so hard to claim that power with my personality, my creative ability, my writing, my crafting, my humor, my people-pleasing, and my niceness. It doesn't really matter why, what matters is, I was seeking all that validation externally by needing more. Needing myself to be more.

External power is anything that comes from outward validation such as praise, money, and recognition. Our desperate desire for external power might manifest itself in a need to control exactly how our body looks, what car we drive, what our partner does or doesn't do, what our children do or look like, how many social media followers we have, how people in a certain community respond to us, or simply wanting one very specific person to do or say certain very specific things for you or about you.

For example, RuPaul, I would like you to look into my eyes and tell me I'm a fierce queen. This would validate my ego. Oprah, I would like you to read my book and deem me a "Thought leader for the next generation!" This would give me external validation for my writing. Twenty-year-old man-boy, I would like you to check me out when I'm driving. This would help me feel sexually relevant. Do you catch my drift?

What external power do you feel like you need to claim?

What external power did you feel you could never get no matter how hard you tried so you simply gave up?

What external power have you shunned because you couldn't get it so you overcorrected? It's most likely stealing all your focus.

I absolutely love verbal affirmation, praise, and gold stars. They are tangible proof of the intangible things I'm wanting external power and validation for. You might not need those, but you might crave gobs of one-on-one time, thoughtful gifts, or people to listen, really listen. For me, I adore compliments. It's why I'm so good at giving them.

But can you even imagine what a recipe for disaster it has been for me to be able to put everything I value about myself and would like validation for—my creativity, my writing, my personality—up for review and approval on not only a daily but hourly basis?

You know that book *When You Give a Mouse a Cookie*? I could use it as the basis of an autobiography called *When You Give a People Pleaser an Instagram*!

But back to the driving question.

What are some of your driving questions?

Here are some ways to identify YOUR driving question. Don't expect yourself to be able to recognize it immediately. But here are some things to look for:

What question do you find yourself asking people you feel close to or confide in?

Example, mine was always in the form of a complaint, "I just don't know what to do!" "What else should I do?"

Which marketing email subject lines, social media quotes, or book or article titles do you gravitate toward?

If a magic fairy could BOP you on the head and give you one answer to one question, what would it be? It's okay if your questions feel messy and clunky. Try to look for themes. Then ask yourself, "What insight can these questions give me about the direction I've been taking my life?"

That's why I love calling it a DRIVING question. That

question is directing your thoughts, and your thoughts are directing your emotions. Your emotions and feelings are steering your actions, and your actions are sure as hell taking you somewhere.

Take a deep breath in. Push that air on out.

Now it's time to let your driving question take you somewhere.

Do you respond to that with an "Obviously." Or do you respond to that with a "I'm not in control of where I'm going, other people are driving." No matter your response, the good news is, you get to choose your focus, and your focus determines your driving question.

Once you've identified your driving question, look at where that question takes you and ask, "Is that really where I want to go?"

My question was in a sense taking me in the direction, professionally and personally, I wanted to go, but it was also capsizing my vessel. Directing me to move and create at a rate that I could never sustain.

Prevent the Spiral

You Can Change Your Driving Question

hen I finally changed my driving question, it changed my entire life. That's how powerful shifting your focus is. That's how powerful focus is. That's the point of all these shifts: they help you shift your focus.

So here's how I changed my driving question.

At the very end of 2014 I was asked to keynote at a conference. And like writing and sharing have always done for me, preparing the presentation helped me to reflect and look at the year as a whole. I'd just finished the Search for Your Awesome tour for Microsoft, and my keynote was also going to be on the focus of how to be awesome.

For one of my slides I got a map of the US and put a little crying emoji on all the cities I visited. Because that's what my Search for Your Awesome tour had felt like. Me frantically sobbing, stressing, and trying to be awesome even though I felt like an underqualified idiot. I wanted to show the group of women I'd be speaking to what seemingly glamorous things often felt like. What reaching your goals felt like, that little crying emoji. How was that possible? I sat there staring at that map. Trying to understand what had happened.

I created another slide that read: HOW CAN I BE MORE AWESOME?

And then in a stroke of what I believe to be divine intervention, I created a follow-up slide with the same phrase with the word *be* crossed out and replaced it with the word *feel*.

And just like that my driving question changed from "How can I be more awesome?" to "How can I feel more awesome?"

It shifted my focus. It helped me see I'd been ignoring my physical and mental health in the ever-frantic search for more. It helped me see my belief that I was never enough, never doing enough, and did not feel like enough.

While working at Hallmark that summer, one of my projects was a little motivational book. Like a tiny poem in book form you could give to someone going through a hard time. I don't think it ever made it to print. But it's where I wrote and realized the concept, "Only you can be you." Which had guided me this far. I knew only Alison could be Alison, but she was trying so hard to figure out how to constantly be better, and it was making me feel worse and worse.

I was looking for a thought to end the presentation on. Something that would reflect what I was just starting to understand. I pulled the truth that had served me and carried me as far as it could for the past seven years, and paired it with a new one that I know will serve me the rest of my life and I hope it will serve you, too:

**Only you can be you, and you're already
as awesome as you need to be.**

I now say this at the end of every podcast episode, coaching session, and keynote. I say it so much that when I share my doubts and fears with friends, or anyone who has heard any of my words, they immediately echo back to me, "You're already as awesome as you need to be."

My driving question is taking me exactly where I want to go, my inner awesome.

You do not need to search for your awesome, your purpose, or that elusive better version of yourself. It's already here, you're living it, you live your purpose in everything you do. Your awesome, your light, love, soul, spirit, Universe, it's in you, it is you. It's guiding you and calling to you. You do not need to be more of anything to access it. You simply need to feel it. You can choose your freaking focus, which is a miracle and one of the greatest gifts you possess.

Every time you return to your focus, and plug back into the power of the whole, you remind yourself you have everything you need in that moment to live your life. It's like you've grabbed the wheel and decided to drive. The craziest part is you stop caring so much exactly where you're going, and focus way more on the joy of getting there.

4

How They Feel Means Nothing About Me!

I'm not offended by all the dumb blonde jokes because
I know I'm not dumb . . . and I also know that I'm not blond.

—DOLLY PARTON

Have you ever been scrolling on social media and every single person that pops up in your feed is so annoying? Maybe every opinion is obnoxious or seems preachy. Maybe it seems like every human you know is upgrading their living space while you're struggling to pay your rent?

But then sometimes the opposite has been true too. You hop on social media and see how great everyone's doing, and how dedicated people are to their causes. "Yay for you!" you chant in your head. "Oh, I love that car for you!" Or even just passing thoughts of, "Aw, they look so healthy and happy!"

What makes these two scrolling experiences so different?

What changed? Did your feed change overnight? Maybe, but probably not. The biggest determining factor of what your experience will be like anywhere you show up, whether it's social media, a restaurant, or even reading a book, is you.

What you bring determines what you get. The glasses you wear color what you see.

If you're feeling small and insignificant, you'll probably bring defensiveness and judgment while you scroll. So everyone online is going to seem annoying. If you're feeling good and just happy to be there, even if the speaker or food at the conference is crap, you'll have a good time.

This makes perfect sense, right? Yet if I tell you that even if your friend walking up to you and saying "You're a bad mom, your kids are jerks to my kids, you're a selfish friend, and I think the way you live is wrong" means nothing about you and everything about her, that how she feels and what she says about you has a lot more to do with her and a lot less to do with you, it's hard to believe.

"But she's watched me parent my kids, she knows me, we go on vacations together . . ." you might say. Still. How she feels about you has nothing to do with you. What she brought to that conversation or your friendship determined what she got.

You might try to argue: "But if I don't listen to her, I'm not taking accountability, I'm unwilling to see myself for who I truly am, right?" No. If you need to take accountability, you should! Apologize, sincerely if needed, be honest with yourself, admit mistakes.

You're not blind to who you really are if you don't listen to people giving feedback from a hurt or defensive place. Not making what people say about you mean anything about you is the kindest, least selfish thing you can do. Seek feedback when you're in a place to receive it, from a professional or from someone with a life you'd want to emulate. Obviously, don't be a monster! That's not what I'm saying. I'm saying other people's interpretation of you is not you. Your interpretation of you is not you.

And this is the mind-blowing shift to tell yourself: *How they feel means nothing about me!* This will take you on a freaking shortcut to feeling your awesome, every single time you use it.

It's not a way to bypass your feelings, it's not saying, "I refuse to change!" It's a reminder to allow the divine awesome in you to see it in everyone else and yourself.

I promise this shift will make you more like a monk than a monster! Trust me, taking things personally used to be my religion. I have the most uncanny ability to make everything about me. (Have you read my book?!) And that's what taking things personally is: it's making everything about you, all the time. Research and your life experience have shown again and again making everything about you is a recipe for misery.

She Can't Be Stopped

I started building my online platform in 2007 with my blog called *She Blogs! She Blogs!* (Yes, named after the hit Ricky Martin song "She Bangs!") Several years after that I morphed my mostly essay-writing blog into one where I also shared about the events I was hosting for my children and a few businesses. I loved using my thematic concept skills mixed with my making-people-feel-good skills to create magical events. In

2010 I thought I was very much on a Martha Stewart trajectory, obviously. Love you, Martha!

Several years after that, Instagram got video capacity. Another one of my natural gifts is my love of nonsense dancing. And when Instagram got video, before flash mobs, and TikTok, and before it was supercommon to see people dancing on the internet who were not professional dancers, I started sharing my slightly offensive hip thrusting with the world. My example of carefree dancing caused a kind of a phenomenon in my community. All of a sudden all these other moms and college girls in Provo, Utah, wanted to dance and party with little ol' me.

So I decided to give the people what they wanted, and also what sounded fun to me, and turn my kind of side hustle blog and Instagram into an events business and throw dance parties. Things escalated quickly.

The parties had themes like "Alison's Shell Yes!: Where Merbabes Dance Their Troubles into Bubbles!" and "Alison's Cabana Boogie," so you can take a vacation from your problems! One of the reasons I believe I'm good at events is because I see them as creating an environment of comfort and ease. I use my empathy cultivated from my extremely anxious nature to anticipate people's needs and feelings. Also I'm wildly flamboyant and would rather have a killer party than save money. All important for good events.

With each party I shifted and expanded. Adjusting and adding more and more. Listening to feedback, using it to make everyone happy. I started the dance parties thinking I was just throwing a party. But people kept asking, "What are you going to wear?!" And then people wanted to see me dance, like I did online. So I started bringing in stages. I'd get up and do a little jig. I remember being pregnant crawling on the floor to "Pour Some Sugar on Me."

Of course I loved it all! Duh! Don't get me wrong, I love the stage! But I just kept thinking that I needed to keep doing what was making the people happy. And the more I did, the more they wanted. It was never, ever enough. Not just for them, but for me. I broke myself over and over to outdo myself, to top myself. The events went from dance parties in a warehouse to Disneyland-like productions in all Utah's best venues. I negotiated all the contracts, brought in all the sponsors, conceptualized their brand activations, and then had a part-time crew and volunteers install it all.

The parties made people feel wonderful because they were freaking fantastic parties! But also because they were a place of love, permission, and light. I allowed them to flow, and be created with joy and passion! So it's kind of confusing how something that came so naturally, and was built with such inspiration and ease, almost killed me. It's why it was so hard to stop.

I Can Control How You Feel— or So I Thought

While I was hosting these parties, which I did over the span of four years, I was falling deeper and deeper into anxiety. I was also happy! When I dance, I get out of my head, and into my awesome. When I plan events, I flow! That's what attracted people. These parties were both killing me and keeping me alive. That's why life is tricky. Because we're not robots who have only one emotion.

But at the height of the events I had a panic attack every single day for at least six months.

Panic attacks were nothing new to me (remember the story of me hiding under my desk in the last chapter?). I had found ways to manage before. But then I got married, had a steady job, and started having babies. The number of people to please, that is, control, and what all their feelings meant about me continued to pile onto my anxiety. I had no full-time staff for these events and it was just too much. My coping tools broke. It was too big. I couldn't control that much, so my body started revolting.

At least once a day for half a year, I would start to hyperventilate and need to find a corner to hide in. I'd cry or pant in the fetal position or pace back and forth until I could get it to pass. When it would get really bad, I'd smack my head against the wall to try to stop my racing thoughts. My old house had a dent in the bedroom wall. I don't know if anyone knew it was from my head whacking it. I would pull at large chunks of my hair, not pulling my hair out, but pulling just hard enough to take the focus away from my racing heart and crawling skin. Then I'd go for a run, or eat a donut, and watch lots and lots of television.

I would figure out how to get to the next day by ignoring every single thing my body was telling me. By dismissing instincts and forcing control. I did not allow my feelings, any feelings, other than anxiety.

I did not get help for a long time and I did not go to therapy. Because, guys, I didn't think my suffering was bad enough for all that! That's truly what I thought.

I had a loving husband and successful event business. People loved me on social media! They applauded me for my growth and creativity. I had healthy kids and nice, well-to-do parents. I had food to eat and a car to drive and I thought I was just being so selfish and dramatic. I just needed to "figure out" how to calm down, I'd think. I needed to figure out how to be more grateful, how to create more value, and then I would feel better. So I kept throwing bigger and bigger parties.

While also always trying to figure out how to lose weight, exercise more, and keep pleasing everybody on social media. This was getting me where I wanted to go. Television stations were reaching out; did I want to pitch a show? News stations were reaching out, businesses and sponsors started coming to me. I just needed to keep going, keep achieving, then I would stop having these panic attacks, right?

I couldn't stop. Why was I so miserable? I couldn't figure it out.

I lost it when I got an email from someone at my most recent event. She was very unhappy about the VIP swag. "I waited hours in line for my free VIP swag and it wasn't worth it," she told me. I refunded her ticket and profusely apologized.

Then I got another email from a girl who was furious that she didn't get one of the free Popsicles that had been available at the party. I refunded her ticket and apologized.

And then I broke.

Who were these people? My dance parties had always attracted gracious, appreciative babes! I felt resentful and so angry with these two women, but I still wanted to make sure they thought I was nice and awesome.

I couldn't see how allowing everyone to have whatever they wanted of me had started to attract people who felt entitled to take and get whatever they could. This drained me; I had no boundaries. So no one respected them. And I constantly felt defensive.

After the Popsicle incident and a run of three dance parties very close together, I was on the couch at my office crying. My very wise childhood friend Jessica Dahlquist, host of the *Extraordinary Moms* podcast, called me.

I unloaded on her.

"I'm doing everything I can and no one is happy! I made the party bigger than I wanted and the tickets cheaper than I wanted, and she is mad about her Popsicle?! I'm breaking my life apart to make everyone happy and it's never enough for them!"

Jessica was kind and patient, but then started giggling. "You know you can't control the feelings of nine hundred women, Alison!?"

She really thought I knew this. But to me it was like a foreign language. Only with Jessica could I be this honest. I said, "But I can. I have a gift for making people feel good. And it's my job to do that."

Then I started sobbing. She immediately stopped giggling because what had been funny to her a moment ago was exactly what had been just about killing me.

"Alison," she said, this time seriously but lovingly, "you can't control the feelings of one person. Let alone nine hundred. You can't control how people feel."

That one sentence sent me on a path that changed everything.

I didn't believe it entirely at first, but I wanted to. It sounded too good to be true. Did I really not have to control how people felt? Could I really not do it even though I thought that's what I had been doing? What God had sent me here to do?! FORCE PEOPLE TO FEEL AWESOME?!

Later I realized the real reason this illusion was so debilitating was because I thought I had to control, that I *could* control, how people felt . . . about me.

I'm Rooting for You in the Life of Your Dreams

he online world and the real world are almost impossibly intertwined. Recently I noticed that a woman I've known, in person, for years, and love stopped following me online. I respect and admire her, and it hurt. Here are just a few of the thoughts I had:

She follows over a thousand people and she consciously chose to unfollow me!? She thinks I'm an idiot, she thinks what I write is stupid. Is it my dancing? She's annoyed by the dancing. She thinks I'm cheesy. What post was it that made her decide I'm crap?

Then I started to shame myself for how much this bothered me. *I hate how much this bothers me!* But here's where it got insane. I thought, *This woman was recently diagnosed with a very severe and advanced form of cancer. I thought we were friends; yes, we haven't talked much in years but I'm loyal! I love her! But she stopped following me online, does she not want me to reach out to her, text her, or leave a comment of support? See, I have her phone number, that changes things, right?*

But her unfollowing me online made me so unsure of our real-life relationship. I was horrified by my uncertainty about reaching out to her. How could this small thing be affecting how I treat another human?! And one who was suffering so much?! But I genuinely felt confused, because I had created a story where she hates me, so should I leave her alone?

But remember, HOW THEY FEEL MEANS NOTHING ABOUT YOU! You can't control people's feelings and you can't take everything personally; I tried it out for you, it sucks. But we do have a choice! What we *can* do is choose a new perspective.

So here are some questions to ask when you're spiraling like I was here, and you want a new perspective:

- How do I feel about myself?

- What is it about this specific person that seems to ruffle my feathers? What am I letting them represent?

- Is this a pattern? Do I repeatedly feel like this?

- What do I value and what is my intention?

I'll answer the questions for this scenario:

- I feel inspired and good about the work I share online. I work hard to tune in, and share what I hope will speak to one heart. Crap. I didn't say how I feel about *myself*! I defended my work. Okay, looks like I still really think I am my work. I accept that. I love myself, I am okay. I am awesome.

- This woman is a really smart, talented artist. She is progressive and represents an intelligent crowd that I often think thinks I'm an idiot. Because I don't take myself too seriously. But I'm not an idiot! So I'm annoyed she might think this, and worried about whether she thinks this. Which means, I still seem to be worried it's true. Hey, Alison. You're not an idiot. And even if you are, you're still awesome!

◎ This is a pattern. I feel this way a lot. So I don't think it has anything to do with her.

◎ I value allowing people to feel how they feel, empathy, understanding, and unconditional love. My intention is to not decide what to do, but to feel that love and allow it to guide me.

And this brought me to, "I'm rooting for you in the life of your dreams!"

I didn't unfollow this woman. I like what she posts. I think it's important to not follow people who trigger you. It's okay to let people go. But in this case I decided that when I saw her posts, I'd say, "I'm rooting for you in the life of your dreams!"

This process reminded me of my intention. I really was rooting for her. From that place of love and flow I knew I'd be guided to reach out if it was needed, and I'd be ready to do it. . . .

Ultimately I did reach out to her. I sent a text and a few messages of love. I prayed for her and her family. And sadly this woman has now passed on. My choice to look for a different perspective has blessed me in sacred ways. I have a piece of her original artwork that I bought at the beginning of her painting career. It's hung in my boudoir and art room and I see it daily. I look at her inspired strokes and offering to the world. And I feel her guiding light as I delve back into my own artistic journey.

Everybody Gets to Be Themselves

I understand how hard it can be to separate how people feel about you from the reality that you already are as awesome as you need to be. I've found mantras to be a helpful way to refocus my thoughts on what is true.

The practice to feel awesome now guides me back to my core:

Feel: Be present, be aware, be the witness.

Awesome: Wake up to my awesome, connect back to my source. I am not these thoughts.

Now: Oh, you mean right now? Okay. Right now. I sense the roof of my mouth, the tension in my arms. Relax. Relax.

Mantras are a technique for returning to flow, to the seat of the soul. And they work when they are rooted to true emotion. Here are a few more mantras that help me remember that *How they feel means nothing about me!*:

- I have all the people I need for this moment.

- I allow myself and the people around me to grow and change.

- It's okay for everybody to grow.

- It's okay for everybody to be themselves.

- I honor the needs of myself and others.

- It's okay to be wrong.

- I can always lovingly moonwalk away.

- I'm still cheering and rooting for you.

- People get to be both. We all get to be both.

If you feel lonely, if you feel like nobody really knows you, if you feel drained like everyone is sucking you dry, if you feel worried that you can't get people to care about you, if you feel like an idiot because you're loud and bubbly, or you don't have the degree, or whatever it is, just know it's okay for you to be yourself. And the more you believe that, the less alone you'll become. The more connected you are to yourself, the more connected you'll feel to the people in your life.

Remember what they all think, whoever THEY are, means nothing about you and your greatness. Look for the people who want you to expand, are cheering for you; look around and appreciate who does that for you. Nurture THOSE relationships, turn to them, and only them for honest feedback about you.

Social media, overidentifying with your work, a follow or an unfollow—none of these things will kill you, but what you make them mean very well could. Don't touch that poison. Put it down. Return to your light, take back your power. What they feel means nothing about you. You are awesome.

5

My True Self
Is Limitless!

Does the sun ask itself, "Am I good? Am I worthwhile?
Is there enough of me?" No, it burns and it shines. Does
the sun ask itself, "What does the moon think of me?
How does Mars feel about me today?" No, it burns, it
shines. Does the sun ask itself, "Am I as big as other
suns in other galaxies?" No, it burns, it shines.

—ANDREA DWORKIN

I remember after I gave birth to my first baby, Ginger, how lost and displaced I felt. My first outing away from my newborn was to get a Diet Coke. So I was in my car driving, a thing regular old Alison did. All alone. Not pregnant, no newborn in sight. And in this solitude for the first time in months, I ached for who I used to be. The Alison who had driven alone in her car so many times before, but didn't have a baby, a whole OTHER human to be responsible for. I had no idea who this new person was. The one with the giant aching breasts and a jaundiced infant at home strapped to UV lights.

I sat at the stoplight almost in shock. Who was I? What was this life? Did I want this life? What had I been thinking?! *It's SO like me to sign up for something huge without much thought!* I lamented. I watched this woman in her forties ride a bike across the crosswalk. I started to cry.

She's probably had a baby! I thought. Then I felt the pain throb from my nether regions after my three full hours of pushing Ginger out. *Will I ever ride a bike again?!* And then I spiraled further. *Am I a person who rides bikes? I don't know! Do I even like bikes?!* For the record, I don't really care about bikes. But I had forgotten!

It's like I thought figuring out if I liked bikes would help figure out who I was. This seems so juvenile! But I've talked to so many people and know that a lot of us feel like we don't know who we are, at least sometimes. And it starts to make us question everything.

Life is always changing things up on us! Pulling the rug out from under us, whether we plan it, like I did with having a baby, or we don't, like when we lose a loved one. All that change can rock our worlds and shake our sense of self. I didn't feel like I could be Diet-Coke-fetching Alison and be mom Alison too. They didn't exist as one.

Who was I? Definitely the hormones but mostly that ego-driven self, the self that believes "Alison" is the girl defined by what she does, says, gets done, or doesn't get done. The girl who works and hustles for her value. The girl who made, and baked, and worked, and moved. That girl had just given birth and couldn't do those things. So now who was she? Who was I?

Is a mom who loses her child no longer a mother? If you're a dancer who can no longer dance, is there no reason to live? If you only see yourself as valuable when you're working, are you of no worth when you lose your job?

And this is exactly why defining ourselves in this way is so problematic. Loving bikes might be one of the ways your soul expresses itself, like flashy nail art, nonsense dancing, and speaking are for me. But they are not me. They are a way I express my light. Take them away and I am still light.

And that light, that inner greatness that you are expressing, it is truly limitless.

The shift *My true self is limitless* invites us to remember who we really are, and what we're actually capable of. It reminds us that we are like the sun, and all we need to do is burn and shine, without question.

You Won't Be a Snotty Sun

Like any of these shifts, it's interesting to note how you initially feel. Does it feel too good to be true that you are limitless? Does it seem childish and naive? How would believing that your true self is limitless serve you? How does it serve those around you?

And in case you're worried that believing you are limitless will make you a snotty sun (what I like to call someone who is full of themselves), I can assure you it will not. Believing you are limitless will not make you arrogant and full of yourself. In fact C. S. Lewis has my favorite definition of humility: "True humility isn't thinking less of yourself, it's thinking of yourself less."

The yapping dog that is our brain is mostly yapping about "I." "I want this! I don't want that! I'm this kind of person who believes this! This is who I am! This is what I stand for!" And other yappy "I" statements of a similar nature.

In a well-known *Harvard Business Review* study[6] that tracked people's use of words, the researcher found depressed people use the word *I* much more often than emotionally stable people. I'm not saying you're arrogant if you're depressed. But rather thinking lowly of yourself is not humility. It will keep you trapped in the loop of self. And in that loop you can only see your limits.

Believing you are limitless will actually make you think about yourself less. You'll spend less energy obsessing on all the things you need to do or say to be yourself, and you'll have more energy to simply let yourself shine.

Consider Your Source

Often when I put my eight-year-old, Rad, to bed, we start talking philosophy. It's his favorite thing to talk about, other than video games I can't understand. My sweet boy is as wise as his freckles are adorable. And one night he asked me, "Mom, how do I know if I'm listening to my heart or God or my mind? Which part do I listen to?"

I told him that was the best question ever and I felt the same way! Then I asked him more about what it felt like inside of him. He thought about it, looked at me seriously, and said, "Mom, I just wish you could see what's inside my head. There are so many parts! There's a part that I call Crazy Town, where anything I think just pops up! I can think TURTLE and *boop!*, there's a turtle. But I just don't know which part is which. You tell me to follow my heart, but which part is that?"

First, it's important to note Rad loves turtles, so they are probably in his heart. But second, I think we all know exactly what he means when he says there are so many parts fighting to be heard inside us. How do we know which is our heart, God, our mind? Which one do we listen to, or try to hear? Which one is the limitless one?

By nature I'm a trusting person. So I tend to give equal weight and trust to all the sources in my life. But as I've built my business and my mental health, I started to realize how important it is to consider the source.

The source being the person you're asking for advice, or the voice inside you you're allowing to influence your decisions.

As a new mom I felt so lost. But which part of me was lost? Was I lost in my heart? Was I lost in my mind? Was I lost from God? Where had I gone? Crazy Town?

Probably. But I wasn't lost and neither are you. You're not lost. You don't not know who you are. You've just set up shop and started listening to the wrong source.

And so to answer Rad's question, how do you know which part is talking? Consider the source.

And how do you consider the source that's coming from within? Listen to the language it uses.

The Language of Limits

You are limitless. Your true, beautiful, glorious essence is Awesome. And yet, the voice that's the loudest, the one we often listen to most, is the one that speaks in limitations and lack.

"It will never work."

"You don't have enough."

"You'll let everyone down."

"You need that degree!"

I've noticed that my ego-driven self, which wants me to believe that I am this world of form, of thought and action, speaks in the very specific language of shame.

Love, the Universe, God, consciousness, your awesome, the core of you that is as expansive and as beautiful as the sun, does not speak in shame. It does not guide you and speak to you with feelings of fear. Read that one more time. Love does not speak in shame. Joy does not speak in shame. God does not speak in shame.

It Doesn't Serve Anyone When You Sit Around Thinking You're a Big Piece of Crap

Speaking of shame, I have a notebook that I created, and the cover reads, "It doesn't serve anyone when you sit around thinking you're a big piece of crap."

It doesn't serve anyone when you feel small. It doesn't serve anyone to believe that you are limited, boxed in, and unable to make a difference! So why do we spend so much time doing it? Why do we listen so closely to the source that wants us to stay small and barks out doubt and fear?

One of the many reasons might be because beating the crap out of ourselves seems to be getting results. And if our value is tied to the results we generate, we seem to not care how we get them. Silly us!

So we shame ourselves into eating healthy, shame ourselves into being nicer to ourselves (think about that), shame ourselves into being "good" whatever that means to us, and shame ourselves into pleasing the people in our life. But shame, which in this case I'll define as believing that we are wrong or bad and that we need to change in order to be worthy, is the language of limits. Limits by nature restrict the size or amount of something. So what are we limiting? Our true nature, our wildest, most glorious selves.

Your shame, your self-hatred, your disgust for yourself will get your results. But as nature and the Bible teach, bad seeds cannot yield good fruit. You can hate yourself into the person you think you should be, but you cannot hate and shame yourself into the person you are truly meant to become. The person this world needs you to become: yourself.

What Makes You, You?

As I was thinking about how displaced we feel after a big change, whether it be emotional, physical, or on a global level like the COVID-19 pandemic, and how hard it is to hear the source of our limitless self guide us, I thought about my friend Lindi.

I met Lindi through her joining my Awesome on Demand community, but she has taught me more than I could ever teach her. Lindi lost her leg in a car accident in 2017, and I've gotten to watch her resiliently shine as she heals. I asked her, "Would you be comfortable sharing what losing your leg did to your sense of self?" Here's what she wrote me:

> When people heard about my leg loss, they wept. They knew how much I loved being active, being outside, randomly dancing, free to move without restrictions. My legs were perfect to me, they took me everywhere

I wanted to go and they were mine. I rarely had
anything bad to say about them. I identified myself as
an athlete, an artist by movement, and someone who is
always up for adventure.

When I woke up without a leg, I sobbed. I thought:
I will never be able to flip again. (I did gymnastics for
fourteen years.) I had just been surfing weeks before
on my honeymoon in Hawaii. And now I couldn't
even sit up without using my hands and needing
help. I couldn't even control when I needed to use the
bathroom. What I thought had made me ME felt like
it was ripped from me. My legs were broken and gone,
and my brain wasn't sounding right. I was covered
with surgical scars, someone else's marks. Something
as intimate as my handwriting no longer looked
like mine.

All the means you use to identify someone felt like
they couldn't be used for me. I was a skeleton of who
I was. And for a long time, I felt that everyone would
have been better off with me dying than watching me
so heartbroken, suffering, and just struggling.

I felt like I couldn't be sad about what happened
because I "was alive."

Time passed and I realized how unhappy I was. I
looked at what I was doing.

I was working at two jobs I hated, not even touching
dumbbells, and drinking till I fell asleep every night.
My new husband and I had split up, we had filed
divorce papers.

I was doing everything in my power to not appear
stupid or less than human because of my traumatic

brain injury and my prosthetic leg. I had felt stupid my whole life at that point. But here I was doing the stupidest thing I could do. Drinking with medications and a fresh TBI. I realized that stupidity doesn't come from someone who tries, it comes from someone who doesn't even show up to try; and I wasn't showing up for anyone, including myself.

I started from scratch and put back things in my life that I knew used to bring me a lot of joy. I had to start small because it was like cleaning wounds, it was painful. Going to the gym was painful. I would walk in thinking I was this big-shot bodybuilder only to fall over just trying to take off my sweatshirt. I left and tried again in a couple days—and wore a zip-up. I started with walking and swallowed my pride.

I wrote this about two weeks ago:

"I do a workout now and it is at the same intensity as it was preaccident. I have realized that my strength didn't come from having two legs. It comes from my soul, it pumps in my blood, and it is powered by my mind. I feel more me than I ever did before."

So what makes me, me?

It is the fighter spirit that never gives up. It is the brave soul that admits when she is wrong, that takes the chances and figures it out later. It is the disciplined daily actions of gratitude. It is the girl who takes a no as still negotiating. I don't need two full legs to do this. I get to be flawlessly Lindi, no matter what my body looks like, how many limbs are there, or how many neurons never connected back in my brain.

It's funny, three years out and the accident has

amplified what I've always loved most about myself. Including BOTH of my legs. I always dreamed about going to the Olympics as a kid. I get an actual chance to do that now with the Paralympics because of them.

I love Lindi's words so much. Isn't she INCREDIBLE? I love seeing the shift when she realized how poorly she was treating herself. And how it wasn't shame that got her up wanting to shine again, but love.

Lindi and her husband ended up staying together, she has the coolest glitter prosthetic leg you've ever seen, and she is currently a professional athlete. She also gifted me a pillow with a jaguar on it, because she's awesome, and it reminds me to trust my resilience and brilliance, just like Lindi.

Think of the words we use to describe feeling stupid. In ABBA's "One of Us" they sing, "One of us is only waiting for a call, sorry for herself, feeling stupid feeling small . . ." Feeling small. We know exactly what that feels like even though it's a size! When we feel bad, sometimes we say, "I want to curl up and die." Shame keeps us small.

Shame has no place in true change and progress. We need accountability, yes! Godly sorrow, ouch it hurts, but yes, too! Reconciliation and amends, of course! Shame is not necessary for any of these things.

Queen Goddess Brené Brown has given us so much. We're so lucky to have her! Her scientific research and findings on shame are truly life and culture changing. She says, "Shame corrodes the very part of us that believes we are capable of change." Amen, Brené.

So how can people meditate, go to church, worship Jesus, follow Buddha, attend spiritual retreats, be committed activists, give money to charity, dedicate countless hours to service, or in every way live honest lives full of good intentions and *still* treat other humans poorly? Still believe that people who are different from them should be counted as less than them? Still feel small and defensive and inferior, and reflect that onto others?

Shame and fear. We allow shame to fuel us and fear to direct our actions. This is yet another reason why it's imperative we commit to the practice of operating from our truest, highest, most expansive awareness. The practice of remembering, you're already awesome. You're a jaguar, so roar!

Don't Poison Your Own Well

Your mind is like your body. You can move it, use it every day, and work it out to exhaustion. But it will never achieve true health if you feed it garbage like fear and shame. Trust me. I've tried. Both for my body and my mind.

When we feel bad, we use those tiny words; we want to collapse, pull our bodies in the fetal position, and shrink away.

But when we feel good? These are some of my words I journaled when I felt GOOD:

> Today I feel HUGE. In a world that wants me to
> be small, small in the volume of my voice, small in
> the size of my body, small in how I think about my
> abilities, and small in how I think about myself, I
> WANT TO BE HUGE. Huge with power, huge with
> enthusiasm, huge with love. I want my hugeness to
> expand in every inch of my clothes, pour out into the
> rooms I enter, and fill others up so they can feel the

greatness of their own power and revel in their own unique hugeness. I didn't start the day feeling this way. I woke up feeling small, fearful, anxious, and overwhelmed. But I took ten minutes to say things I'm grateful for, and changed my mind's state by moving my body. I listened to music that fills me with joy. It doesn't always work to keep the demons at bay. But today it did. And now I'm going to be large and in charge. Here's to being huge.

Why do gratitude, exercise, and music work to help us feel expansive and good? I know, I know there's a ton of research on this. But on a spiritual level, these things invite us out of our small self, and into our awesome. Into our connected hugeness. The hugeness that, like the sun's rays, seems to have no end. They give us a glimpse of how we are in truth, as radiant and brilliant as that ball of incandescent gas.

But like I journaled, these things don't *always* work, right? I've gone on my fair share of runs that have simply resulted in me crying in a patch of grass on the side of the road. I've meditated myself into a deeper depression.

They don't always "work" because they aren't meant to be used as drugs, though that's how we often treat them and use them. *I feel anxious—better go for a run and in twenty minutes I'll feel better.* Like a drug, it will work only temporarily if it works at all. It will work until you remember the stupid thing you said or the mean thing someone else said. It works until you go back into your mind, your thoughts, your form.

Unless we actively engage in our loving awareness and identify the source that's directing us, we'll only ever get temporary fixes. If we want to operate from our hugeness and our expansiveness more of the time, we have to stop poisoning our own wells with the belief that we are small and need to change and be different in order to be valuable. You're already awesome.

You Can Break the Cycle

I can kind of quickly spiral when I go to write about any of my shifts. *I Quickly Spiral*, yet another fabulous title for my memoirs! But I quickly spiral when I write them for the world, because I try to apply them to every scenario. In my gut, in my awesome core, I know that they are true principles; I've applied them, I've taught them, they've changed my life, and as I've established, it's not like they aren't taught in different forms everywhere. Still, as I write the shift *My true self is limitless* I quickly spiral when I think about the different cycles. Cycles like poverty, abuse, ancestral trauma—there are so many cycles. And they are topics I feel insanely inadequate to start to grapple with.

How does thinking *My true self is limitless* help someone who is worried about access to clean water!? Is it not something that applies to everyone? I try to dissect it all in my mind. And then I pause, take a breath, try to sink into the awareness that I'm being directed by my thoughts, and then I spiral back into, *See! I can't stay present and surrender! No one should listen to me!*

My husband, Eric, keeps reminding me it's not my job or responsibility to solve the entire world's problems. One night when I was starting to panic, yet again, that no one will understand what I'm trying to say, he said, "Babe, you're just telling people they're awesome. You're not Einstein introducing the theory of relativity!"

And this perfectly highlights the duality that is me, and I'm pretty sure a lot of us. I have the audacity to believe that I should be able to solve the entire world's problems, the audacity to seek out an agent and a book deal, the tenacity to actually follow through on it all, and at the same time I'm pretty sure I've just tricked everyone. We believe that we should have our wildest dreams, while simultaneously feeling unworthy of them.

Some people like to just label this as "impostor syndrome," and others might point out it means you're not a sociopath or a narcissist. But it doesn't change the fact you feel crappy, right?

But here's what I know: it's very difficult to break any cycle, but awareness, a recognition that there *is* a cycle, and breaking that first link in the chain are always integral steps. How can we break any cycle if we either won't recognize there is one or can't see that there's one?

Though of course telling people that they are inherently whole, and that they are already as awesome as they need to be, might not be as complicated as the theory of relativity, what if it is? What if it's harder to believe for ourselves? What if it seems just as abstract and messy?

Yes, a huge part of the cycle of abuse, addiction, and poverty is of course not having access to resources, but what if another huge part of it is keeping people believing that they can ONLY be victims of the cycle? Or even worse, that the cycle is their only reality?

History has time and time again proven the power of one person standing up and saying, "Why not me? Why not now?"

Absolutely, many people have more limits put on them for a variety of reasons. There is study after study that confirms this. In no way do I want to dismiss that truth or say it's easy to make any of these shifts. It won't be! But I always go back to the questions, Do I believe that if all people felt this shift was true the world would be more loving? And would people be bolder in their truth, and kinder in their actions?

If more people could interrupt their cycles of not believing there's a reality for them beyond the one they can see right now, and use that as a north star of hope, would it serve not only them but the people in their community? Do I believe this is true?

Um. Yeah. I freaking do. So my true self is limitless, I am limitless, which in my book means you are too. Every time we remember this we start to break out of a limiting cycle. When we break out of that cycle more solutions appear to us, and a well of infinite resources swells around us.

> **Prevent the Spiral**

TAP It Out to Stop the Cycle of Shame or Blame

Remember, deciding to feel awesome and knowing it's already your truth is not about feeling fantastic all the time. It does, however, invite us, when we start to feel like crap, to lean back and observe. This is how we can tap into our true self. Usually when I'm in a cycle of shame or blame, I just need to feel my fear, anger, or sadness. Let me walk you through an example.

TUNE IN: I'm spiraling. I feel depleted. I feel hopeless. This writing isn't going how I hoped it would, and now I'm pretty sure I'll reach no one and it's all crap. I thought my true self was limitless but apparently it's not because I can't get her to show up.

Then I tune in some more. What's one word for all this? Fear.

This helps break my negative thought spiral. I become aware of the spiral rather than diving into it. Oh, hey, spiral of fear. I see you.

ACCEPT: I say, "Oh, hey, fear, thanks for trying to keep me safe! You feel terrible. But apparently you need a moment, so let's do this. You're valid. You're trying to keep me safe again. Let me check; no, still not in any physical danger. But thank you for your concern."

Sometimes this is enough for it to lift. Sometimes I decide I'm going to be afraid and do it anyway. In both cases, no repressing or bossing around the fear. Just accepting it.

PICK MY FOCUS: My true self is limitless. Why on earth am I trying to contemplate and fathom my limits from a place of fear? I choose the focus that my offering of words, my best, my truth, is enough. I am enough. No amount of right or wrong words will change that.

I always sprinkle in gratitude if it feels authentic. Meaning the fear feels like it's passing through me and I'm not shoving it down. When I feel the fear start to dissolve, I can see that I'm grateful I get to share my truth. I'm grateful to be doing work that is meaningful to me. I'm grateful to know all of it is an expression of my true self, and my true self is limitless.

It is an act of courage, love, and creative genius to embrace your physical, mental, and emotional circumstances and know that, yes, THEY might be limits, but the core of you, your awesome, is limitless. And like Lindi, we can look for the bursts of light in our storms. She told me:

> The accident left a lightning bolt scar on my leg. I think it's God's little omen for me. It's a great responsibility to wear my weakness out in the open. I get to remind people that you can be broken, and priceless. That the sky is still beautiful with all its storms, and guess what? Storms have lightning!

6

I Am Exactly Where I Need to Be!

Be patient with yourself.
Nothing in nature blooms all year.

—OLD PROVERB

At the end of 2017 I had been preaching, teaching, and believing "Only you can be you, and you're already as awesome as you need to be!" for years, focusing on feeling awesome rather than being awesome. I had changed my driving question, I was headed where I wanted to go, and I was genuinely changing.

I stopped a lot of my frantic action. I had stopped giving what I didn't have to give. That was the year I allowed myself to stop doing dance parties, even though that disappointed a lot of people. Instead I launched my *Awesome with Alison* podcast, started creating my Year of Awesome calendar, which turned into my online coaching group, Awesome on Demand, and I also started growing and scaling my Build an Awesome Brand workshop. I had lost lots of weight by counting calories, controlling and restricting that aspect of my life and my body, but allowing myself to flow almost everywhere else.

I felt good! So good! I chose faith in my inherent wholeness over praise. I mean, at least more often than I used to. I chose belief in the importance of a greater good, over me needing to be seen as good. I chose projects that fueled me rather than drained me. I stopped trying to grow on social media to prove my value to myself or others.

It wasn't all easy breezy in 2017; in fact, some of the hardest things of my life had also happened that year. We lost my infant nephew Gavin a few months earlier on Eric's side of the family. It was, and still is, devastating. And on my side of the family we were learning to live with the blow of my dad's recent incurable cancer diagnosis, which he had also gotten that year. I had spent a week with him in the hospital after his stem cell transplant—which thankfully, to this day, is still keeping his cancer at bay. My dad and I had worked together from his hospital bed on my Build an Awesome Brand workshop when he felt well and focused enough.

And even with these hardships, new 2017 Alison had it all locked down! From this place of strength and contentment, I remember thinking, *Oh no! I think I'm getting so well-balanced people won't be able to relate to me! I have it all figured out, I guess! I hope I can stay relatable!*

Yes, that was an actual concrete thought I had. Silly Alison.

I had just signed the biggest contract I'd ever gotten for something I just loved, coaching and consulting, and five days before Christmas in 2017, I went on a run, more specifically a gratitude run, in which I focus on and list things I'm grateful for as I run, because I was feeling overwhelmed with the holiday season, work, and all the to-dos piling up.

On that run, I was feeling a bit anxious and stressed, but I knew by the end of it I'd be ready for my big meeting! I'd make it through the holiday season, and 2018 would be incredible.

Little Did She Know

I saw the car as it took the corner turn too quickly, veering into the extrawide shoulder of the road that acts as a sidewalk because there isn't one. I didn't even have time to finish the thought *That car will st—?* before it hit me.

There was nothing I could have done. My eyes were facing forward, I was on the "correct" side and part of the road for a runner. I couldn't have jumped out of the way or dodged it. It happened too fast. It was small blond runner versus sedan, and the sedan, with its driver who hadn't seen me, won.

I remember the impact. The impact—the feeling of steel hitting my body—it was otherworldly. But I don't remember how the car hit me, where it hit me, how I landed, how far back I flew, or any of the other juicy details that people thoughtlessly ask when they want a clearer picture.

I had flashbacks about the impact of the car hitting me for years, though thankfully I don't get them as much anymore. The impact left me motionless on the December frozen black asphalt. I couldn't move anything. I didn't want to move anything.

My body was in shock, and I just remember trying to gauge my level of injury by watching the pool of blood that was growing around my head. Blood was steadily streaming from an open wound near my right eyebrow, and it was oozing down across my face as I lay on my left side.

The driver tried to talk to me, she seemed distant and faceless. She was frantic and also in shock. And for a moment I just watched the blood keep pooling. It was getting bigger and bigger. A shiny dark red puddle surrounding me like a halo. And after a while, and still unable to move, I clearly remember my assessment was this:

Honestly, Alison, it's not that much blood. Stop being dramatic. You're fine. You can make your three o'clock meeting.

WHOOMP, THERE IT IS!

It wasn't until weeks later that I understood what it had taken a car smacking into me to realize: just how incredibly ruthless I was to myself.

It's like I had been violently beating the crap out of myself my whole life, but in the last few years had shifted to a less abrasive model of abuse. Just some light bullying, forcing, and shaming with the occasional shove.

The pain I remember, waking up the next morning and saying, "I feel like I was hit by a car . . ." only to remember, "Oh wait, I was." The black eye and bruises I remember too. But the shame. Looking back I mostly remember the shame.

While bleeding on the ground, and for days after, I felt so much shame. Shame that they called an ambulance, "No, no, it's okay, just call my husband," I had said.

Shame that the paramedics had to help me when I passed out in the ambulance. Shame that my CT scan revealed broken ribs, a fractured vertebra, but nothing more severe. So I probably shouldn't have wasted their time.

I was so worried about if I had been friendly enough to the

doctors, if I'd been nice enough to the girl who had hit me, who was in as much shock as I was.

"You hit me," I remember saying to her from the ground as she watched me bleed unmovingly. She stood frozen in fear, not knowing what to do. "You need to be more careful," I told her. It wasn't angry or explosive. I could barely talk after all, but it was more like how I scold my kids. "Look both ways! Be careful!" I remember apologizing for saying the f-word, so I think I must have said it at some point. Sounds like me!

I felt shame for my joking with the doctor as he stitched up my head, because he also had left me without any instructions on what to do next other than, "Don't sit still too much with broken ribs, you'll get pneumonia. And come back on Christmas to get the stitches out." I must have made him think I was in the ER for drugs, I concluded. That's why he didn't prescribe me any and I was in excruciating pain.

I had shame for what I posted on social media that day. Me with two thumbs-up saying I had been hit by a car but I was going to be okay! And I felt deep defensiveness and anger toward anyone who didn't see my pain.

I was berating myself and stuck in so much shame not feeling injured enough to warrant an ambulance ride, and then felt like my shame was confirmed when hours after being struck by a literal ton of metal, I got a text that essentially said, "Just be grateful you're not dead." Here's a thought, the next time you're beating yourself up for having a hard time: if we only get to feel like our suffering is valid if we're dead, it's time to reevaluate the standard.

Shockingly, I did not make my three o'clock meeting. I was taken by ambulance and set on a path to heal that took nearly three years. The injuries affect my body to this day.

Right after my accident, I sat in bed for weeks and months, frustrated and furious to still be in pain from my broken ribs and fractured vertebra. I would watch myself starting to beat myself up for not getting more done. Being lazy, healing too slowly. But luckily I had learned how to watch my thoughts, not just have them. And that's when I realized I was in an abusive relationship with myself.

By never allowing myself to believe *I'm exactly where I need to be*, I never got to be where I was. This is the sixth shift, and it took getting hit by a car for me to learn it.

I was never okay holding still. I was never okay to rest or to slow down. I had to be somewhere else, get somewhere else, be someone else. Be better, be different, be both bigger and smaller. Older and younger. Make sure everyone was happy while I tried to move to the next thing. And I guess I thought shame and force were the most efficient ways to do that.

People who just meet me, or have seen me online, seem to be shocked when I say I'm both wildly confident and also tortured with ruminating and self-flagellation. I'm both anxious and deeply in the flow. But different areas of our life, different relationships, they expose different parts.

I had spent the past four years being so much nicer and forgiving of myself that I thought I was crushing it with self-compassion. But the compassion was only there because everything was how I wanted it in the areas I wanted it. My body, my business, my family. I had them where I needed them to be, or directed toward where I demanded they go. So I was okay. I also had a steady quantifiable incline in all the numbers that reported success back to me, such as podcast downloads and my income.

But the abusive mean girl was still present. She was just lulled into quiet for a bit, and not as overtly severe. Almost more insidious in her covertness. She was outed by the smack of that sedan.

I'm right here with you, watching all the media reflect back to us and fuel our belief that we need to do more to be more. That we're not enough as we are. We should figure it out! Be somewhere else! Which is why I say with total and complete confidence: almost everyone is in some form of an abusive relationship with themselves. We have such a hard time believing *I'm exactly where I need to be*.

Want proof? My top-performing content piece of all time is a fifteen-second clip where I'm marching and clapping to my own beat as I sing a made-up song (that I often sing to myself) to camera, which goes like this:

"You are doing a really good job, a really good job, a really good job! Yes YOU! Are doing a really good job, even if you're just sitting in your bed watching television!"

The number of comments I get weekly of people saying they sing this to themselves or someone else would floor you! But it makes so many people feel better because we believe that in order to BE good we need to DO good, which is why my nonsense song of "You are doing a really good job!" is such a relief. We desperately want to believe it, but it's so freaking hard.

Trusting You Are Where You're Meant to Be Keeps You from Getting Stuck!

I did a podcast interview about six months after my accident and the interviewer asked me a lot of questions about what I'd learned. After sharing all the incredible lessons I was in the middle of learning, she said, "I'd say you're glad you got hit by a car!"

Listen, I wouldn't say I'm glad I got hit by a car, but I am incredibly grateful for all the good, and even the hard, realizations that came from it. I don't think we need to be happy or excited about any of our hard experiences or past traumas; we simply need to accept them and allow them, like every single experience does, to teach us what they can. When we allow ourselves to say "I'm exactly where I need to be," we can see the lessons emerge and allow our souls to journey in a life-affirming direction. Knowing you are awesome exactly where you are actually prevents you from staying stuck. For when the student is ready the teacher appears.

Did I manifest or attract being hit by a car? Was it karma, was it God's plan? You're all going to have your own beliefs on that, and my job, I'm learning, is simply to be okay with that and know what my beliefs are. I believe, like Rumi says, "What you seek is seeking you." I was seeking peace, I was seeking relief, I was seeking a deeper relationship with myself that was based on unconditional love. I got what I was looking for. But note, that perspective is a choice. And that's why we are such powerful creators.

We create the meaning of any circumstance, that's our role as the creator of our lives.

I believe that this moment, the one right here, the only one we have, is the perfect teacher. And when we allow ourselves to believe *I'm exactly where I need to be*, we surrender to the moment and can more clearly see what it has to teach us.

If I had said "I'm exactly where I need to be" and felt the pain and fear in that moment, I might not have carried it with me for so long afterward. Again, I have no regrets. They were the exact lessons that got me here. And right here is freaking awesome.

I'm Doing Awesome

I titled this book *You're Already Awesome*, because we do not need to "do" or "be" awesome; we are inherently, unquestioningly, unconditionally awesome. However, it's tough to change the programming that I must always be "doing" and "doing a good job!" So I always try to reach myself, and others, right where they are. This is why I continually tell myself and others, "I'm doing awesome," with the knowledge that how I'm "doing" doesn't mean anything about me or anyone else. It still feels good and encourages me to keep going.

I have tumblers with "I'm doing awesome!" printed on them and I kept one by my bedside the weeks after my accident when I lived mostly in bed. I'd take a sip of water and say, "I'm doing awesome at healing." I would tell myself, *I'm exactly where I need to be* as I worked toward self-compassion and acceptance, even when I wasn't achieving and "doing."

"I'm doing awesome resting," I'd say. "I'm doing awesome allowing other people to help me," I'd affirm. "I'm doing awesome sitting still and slowing down," I'd say, even if I didn't believe it. I'd say it until I could feel it. Like a loving friend to myself. "I'm exactly where I need to be."

I did what I needed to do that year after my accident in my work and life. Again, I know it's what I needed to do because it's what I did. I did allow myself to rest, but I got back to work (albeit on muscle relaxers) by March.

Determined to be kinder to myself, I got a trauma therapist, as I'd never not insist a close friend of mine do the same. But I also traveled a ton that year. My healing happened in stages. And for almost the first year postaccident I felt positive and patient, at least patient for me. But as the one-year anniversary loomed, I sunk lower and felt more and more physical pain.

I remember crying in frustration to Eric. "This has set me back! I'm so sick of it! I was on such a good trajectory, things were finally coming together! And now I'm getting fat and my business is messy and everything hurts. I still can't run." I sobbed and sobbed. He said to me, "I know you feel like you got knocked back, but I swear I can see how you've actually been launched forward. You'll feel it someday."

Still I was so frustrated. How had it been a year and things weren't better!? I'd felt my damn feelings, I'd been grateful, I had a therapist! I was DOING A GOOD JOB! Why did I feel like I couldn't get out of bed or put up Christmas decor? The second the weather got colder I started having more flashbacks. They were so weird and disorienting. I was sick of not being mad about my accident. It had been a year, that's all the patience I was willing to give! I was pissed and sad and I sunk into a depression.

And yet, I was exactly where I needed to be.

I gained weight, the weight I had been so proud to have kept off despite not being able to exercise. I watched as this weight gain showed me how I really felt about my body. It uncovered another layer of what RuPaul always refers to as "the inner saboteur."

Mine would hiss, *People will be disappointed in you. They'll see you're a failure because of this weight. No one will trust you or want to learn from you.* Even if I liked how I looked, even if

I knew I was just fine, I'd get those inner messages, saying, *You can't be successful and have the life you want if you gain weight.*

That belief had been buried so deep inside me I'd never been able to see how flawed it was. I had never been able to see it so clearly and objectively so that I could observe it and say, "Let's work on letting that go."

I was exactly where I needed to be.

In my depression, and after a year of constant pain and headaches, I did something I'd never done before, I sought out solutions for my health and didn't give up. I made doctor appointment after doctor appointment and kept them! I found a phenomenal physical therapist. It took hours and hours and months and months, it drove me crazy with how slow the progress was. But my physical therapist and his questions helped me realize how much I had ignored my body my whole life. Refusing to listen to her needs and only ever trying to dominate and control her. I learned to listen to her pain.

I was exactly where I needed to be.

Just Because It's Hard Doesn't Mean You're Doing It Wrong

Healing, growing, learning, and expanding. They are all messy, nonlinear, often painful processes. As Jimmy Eat World teaches in "The Middle":

"It just takes some time, Little girl, you're in the middle of the ride, everything, everything will be just fine!"

Just because it's hard doesn't mean you're doing it wrong. Being depressed and hitting my breaking point with migraines and neck pain was part of my process. I was doing awesome.

Working hard to be positive for a year, and then feeling like I lost ground, when I was ready to feel more difficult feelings, was part of the process. Writing this three years postaccident I can clearly see I was in the middle of the ride.

I wrote this exactly one and a half years after being hit as I came out of my depression:

> Last week I realized most of this year has been a lot of RAMPING UP to be able to get through what I must.
>
> No matter how much I "recharged" I felt depleted. I could objectively see things not getting done—hobbies, dishes, cleaning, exercise, mundane LIFE things, but it's like I have just been watching them float by. I finally realized I've been in a bit of a depression . . . for most of 2019. I thought it was bad habits or laziness. But now I can see clearly, it was the fog. It's tricky like that. I go through these cycles (ones of depression and anxiety) a lot in my life. It's hard to tell from the outside because I still work and live, I still laugh and smile and it's all true. It's just the EFFORT required to do it can feel unbelievably impossible.
>
> But for the first time I feel like I've made it through a cycle with compassion for myself. It's a huge victory. I allowed myself to be down a lot. Be in bed a lot. Watch TV more. Eat treats and not feel shame. I leaned into what I thought was "laziness or bad habits," but didn't fight them too hard. And now at last I feel things starting to lift.
>
> The point of all this self-help, mantras, gratitude practices, feel-as-awesome-as-you-are STUFF that I create and share is NOT so I (or you) will never

feel anxious or depressed. That took me a minute to REALLY GET. The POINT is to make it through the cycles ALIVE. Really alive. To ease inevitable suffering, and when possible STOP self-imposed suffering.

Right now as I wake up and ease back into life, I'm not trying to do anything but exist. No forced feelings or intentions. Just breath and connection. I'm enjoying being able to feel lighter. I'm enjoying being able to SEE my kids and husband with happier eyes. It's a beautiful life I couldn't see for a while. I appreciate it so much.

I guess I'm just saying hi. I see you through the fog. Your fog or mine. You're absolutely stunning in it. Sit in it. Or quit for a minute. Be kind to your foggy self. You are exactly where you need to be. And so am I. Life is cyclical, we don't have to fight to make it summer all year round. There's still plenty of love and beauty in the darkness, and it never stays dark forever.

DAMN! That's a woman who isn't beating the shit out of herself quite so much. Who has a loving relationship with herself even when she's not doing all the things she thinks she needs to do. That's a woman who knows her inner greatness. Yes, she's me, and she's exactly who I want to be.

Believing *I'm exactly where I need to be* invites us to feel awesome wherever we are because it reminds us we are not victims who are beholden to outside circumstances. We can decide to feel and own our inner greatness and power even in our pain and allow it to guide us through.

How to Embrace Being Exactly Where You Are

Y ou don't need to be hit by a car to know what it feels like to metaphorically be hit by a car. A cancer diagnosis, the loss of a loved one, the ending of a relationship. An illness, a surgery, unprocessed trauma that pops up during a world pandemic. A faith transition, a spiritual awakening, a moral inventory. They can all have a severe, disorienting impact. Using the shift *I'm exactly where I need to be* is an incredible tool to feel awesome when you don't know which way is up. It invites you to:

TUNE IN: Notice where you are physically, mentally, and emotionally.

ACCEPT: This is where I am. This is how I feel. It's okay. It's where I need to be.

PICK YOUR FOCUS: What does this moment, the only moment I have, want to teach me?

Here's a few ways you can work on embracing that you are exactly where you need to be.

Baby-step it. The more you do reps with the shift of believing *I'm exactly where I need to be*, in light, easy ways, the stronger your muscles will be for the big, tough stuff.

> When waiting in a long line: I'm exactly where I need to be.

> When spending time with a loved one: I'm exactly where I need to be.

> When having an uncomfortable feeling: I'm exactly where I need to be.

> When you feel super overwhelmed with the deadline of a project: I'm exactly where I need to be.

> When you feel like you're too old, too far behind, or not where you want to be in your career: I'm exactly where I need to be.

> When you're resting, healing, depressed in bed, having a panic attack: I'm exactly where I need to be.

Reassign your habits. It was a gift that I had lots of healthy habits before I was hit. But they almost all involved a healthy, high-functioning body.

This is one of the reasons physical ailments can be so mentally depleting. You used to be able to do something to feel better, and now you can't. I couldn't run, I couldn't serve others, I couldn't dance. I felt so fuzzy with painkillers and brain injury. So I did what I could. I reassigned my habits. I traded gratitude runs for gratitude baths. I would sit in the tub and as the water filled up I said things I was grateful for out loud.

I decided to allow myself to serve others by allowing them to serve me. My friend Ashley, who runs her own business, selflessly came to my bed and helped me launch the products I had scheduled to launch in January, like my calendar and coaching group. Again, my husband and I are both self-employed and that income was desperately needed. Friends wrapped my kids' Christmas gifts and my mom flew up even when I said she didn't need to. I accepted. I allowed. I was grateful.

Rest. I now know rest is part of a cycle that makes me whole. So I reassigned all that positive self-talk I had reserved for when I was doing awesome by getting lots done, by allowing myself to believe the same as I rested and healed.

"Rest is its own excuse and warrants no further explanation. Love is a life anchored in rest," writes Dr. Saundra Dalton-Smith in her beautiful book *Sacred Rest*.[7]

I tell myself I'm doing awesome all day every day. "You're doing a great job, doing your crappiest version of your best!" I say when I unconsciously start to get down on myself.

Believe that your pain is valid because it's yours. Since sharing this story I've talked to dozens of people who have been hit by cars and have lost limbs and been in the hospital for months. They reach out to me with emails, come up to me after speaking events and workshops. They cry and thank me for sharing what happened. It made them feel less alone, helped them understand their experience deeper. I talked to one woman who told me how she had gone through a divorce because of being hit by a car; she now felt heard and seen. I've talked to my friend who was nearly stabbed to death about flashbacks and healing, and I've listened to loved ones and friends who have lost children in horrific ways share their grief, and we all feel connection as we hold space for one another.

And do you want to know the craziest thing? Not a single

one of these warriors has looked at me and said, "Your pain is nothing compared to mine, Alison. How dare you?"

They've grabbed me in their arms, cried with me, listened to me, and thanked me for sharing my struggles with my trauma. I try to be ridiculously careful to never rate or rank my accident, or make it seem more severe than it was. It was pretty crappy, and sure, it could have been worse. But here's the thing, it can literally ALWAYS be worse.

We don't have to live in our pain, attach to it, and make it define who we are. "We are the music makers. And we are the dreamers of dreams."[8] We create meaning, we are creators! But acknowledging and allowing your pain does not make you ungrateful, negative, or bad. Living in it will make you miserable, and if you don't allow it to pass through it will consume you.

Even if your pain seems small. Even if well-meaning people tell you, "You're lucky you're not dead." Your pain is valid. Your trauma needs to be felt so it can be freed.

Allowing yourself to believe *I'm exactly where I need to be*—feeling what I need to feel, in the body, in the space I need to feel it—will begin to set you free.

Just remember that you are NOT your pain or your trauma. As Moana sings to the fire monster Te Kā, as she realizes Te Kā is also the benevolent island goddess Te Fiti, "You know who you are."[9]

You are love, light, truth, God, spirit, you are Awesome. Find the meaning your suffering is showing you, but remember it doesn't mean anything about you.

The shift of *I'm exactly where I need to be* allows you to accept that you're awesome and in a wash of unconditional love. Unconditional love means regardless of any action or outcome, I will love you. I will love myself where I am, no matter what.

It's a decision, that's it. One we practice by making it again and again no matter what is thrown at us, or what mistake we or others make. We seek after this frantically because we refuse, yes, freaking refuse to give it to ourselves, when, ironically, the only person you need unconditional love from is yourself.

When we have it we feel whole. We are free. We flow and are guided, we serve the greatest good.

You are incredible in this moment. You are doing a really good job. And you are exactly where you need to be.

7

Feeling My Feelings Sets Me Free!

Don't fight the feeling, invite the feeling!

—BRUNO MARS

My sister and I had this giant beanbag chair we used to fight over. It had a chocolate-brown microsuede cover and was the expensive fancy kind of beanbag that was the envy of any dorm room or college apartment. It was perfect for two coeds to get swallowed by for intimate movie watching. The only reason we had such a luxury piece of furniture as college students is because we had stolen it from our parents, and every six months or so one of us would recruit some friends to help us reclaim the LoveSac from the other sister's apartment. We always lived close, but not in the same complex.

It took at least three people to move it and you needed a truck. That thing was huge and heavy! But it was my turn to reclaim the sac, so I convinced my boyfriend and a few roommates to join me and we headed to Andrea's apartment.

Growing up I was always teased, nicely and not, for my occasional outbursts only witnessed by family or close friends. My parents called them meltdowns, my friends called them freakouts. Looking back I think they were often panic attacks. But it's hard to tell, right? I've always been insanely expressive. I feel a lot of feelings and my face shows what I feel even when I don't want it to. When I wasn't being careful, or watching myself, I'd get too big, too loud. I'd notice when I could see it on people's faces. The disgust. The disgust with my big feelings. The slight embarrassment, or wanting to look away. I could see them visibly lean back, put some distance between us. I didn't have violent outbursts, just expressive outbursts.

When you're the person having the outburst, detecting disgust will often cause you to do one of two things. The first option is to get bigger, get louder, freak out more, and make sure people understand all the feelings you cannot seem to grasp or understand yourself. The second option is to shut it all down. I could usually shut it down in public, monitor myself to not get too big, be too expressive, or too loud. But the people I was closest to, mainly my family, would see more. Yelling, pacing, heavy breathing. I dated a few guys in high school and early college, and one semiseriously my freshman year, but my boyfriend at this time, he was my first love. The only boy I'd ever been openly and fully myself around.

We'd been dating for a few years at this point, the point when we went to steal the beanbag. My friends and I burst into Andrea's apartment. She was there and a brawl, good-natured but intense, ensued. Andrea and some roommates piled on the bag, I leapt on top of them and pushed them off. Everyone was laughing and yelling.

I shouted orders to my boyfriend, "Open the door! Grab the bag! GO GO GO!"

Not feeling as comfortable as two sisters to grapple it out, our roommates faded to the background, leaving Andrea and I crawling on each other. There were no tears or scars or bruises. Just raw emotion pouring through me as we conquered and dragged the monolith-like beanbag through the halls of the apartment complex.

Was my intensity far beyond that of everyone else? I'm sure I didn't think so, but objectively, and knowing me, it probably was.

I remember catching the eye of my boyfriend as I shouted final words of triumph to Andrea while loading the beanbag in the car. He was absolutely horrified. I saw the disgust I hated to see when I was a child now on his face; he was disgusted with my raw emotion. I was too big. It was too much.

Of course like most early twentysomething girls, I understood this to mean I was disgusting. That I was too much and it was something I needed to apologize for. I mean, how awful it must have been for him to see me have big emotions, right?

Isn't it funny, how vividly this memory has stuck? How much it has hurt. I've never shared it publicly. Writing it was uncomfortable and painful, bringing back those feelings of shame I felt in the hall, seeing the man I loved look at me that way.

His response tapped into one of my deepest wounds. The wound that Alison is just TOO MUCH.

So here's the thing about feelings and emotions: There's a lot of debate about different models of classification, and debate about which feelings are core emotions and what's to be done with them. Regardless of what you label them, there's a universal consensus that feeling your feelings is absolutely necessary. And as the title of the insanely incredible and heartbreaking bestseller touts, when we don't process our trauma and feel our feelings, *The Body Keeps the Score.* Meaning, what goes in must come out, and not feeling our feelings can be insanely detrimental to not just our mental, but our physical health.

In it, Bessel van der Kolk, MD, says:

> The more people try to push away and ignore internal warning signs, the more likely they are to take over and leave them bewildered, confused, and ashamed. People who cannot comfortably notice what is going on inside become vulnerable to respond to any sensory shift either by shutting down or by going into a panic—they develop a fear of fear itself.[10]

You Are a Feelings Idiot

And yet most of us are feelings idiots. I said it. It's the only time I'm going to be harsh with you: there's a very good chance you're a feelings idiot! But you're in good company.

I didn't think I was one. I mean I have so many feelings! I have such big feelings! I can sense what other people are feeling and, like a ninja, decipher and detect the emotions around me.

And yet, this did not make me immune to being a feelings idiot.

We tend to choose certain emotions or feelings and live there. It's an emotional habit. People who get angry will get angry about things. People who get sad will get sad about things. It doesn't matter what the exact circumstances are.

Think about it, what's your emotional habit? It might be to detach, to numb, to shut down. Mine is anxiety. I use my anxiety like a drug. It numbs the true feelings, it keeps me busy and moving. It gives me a sense of control, even if it also makes me absolutely miserable.

I have hormonal and chemical imbalances, and those also cause anxiety. But years of observing and practicing how to feel awesome now has helped me to notice the difference between the habitual and the hormonal anxiety. And even my hormonal anxiety has been greatly helped by every single idea I share in this book.

I challenged myself at the outset of writing this book to enjoy the process. That the measure of my success would not be books sold, or even hearts touched. I cannot control those things, so I do not make them my goal. My goal was to write the book in joy with ease, writing heart to heart. Allowing my words to be guided by love, and not by fear and wanting to control how I'm perceived.

To remind myself to keep this the focus, I put this message on a lightboard that greets me at my office: "Live in the flow and air hump as you go." To me it means: surrender, have faith, have fun, and be your air-humping self while you do it. It has been my guiding intention.

I haven't been able to enjoy many of my successes. I didn't get to bask in the tininess and wonder of my babies, or feel proud of myself for a job well done almost ever, because of anxiety. A lot of my life all other emotions were felt only briefly, as I fell back into the hellish comfort of the devil I knew. With this project I felt ready to challenge myself to do this huge seemingly insurmountable task, without being fueled by my favorite drug.

It required every single shift that this book is composed of, and it required me to use these shifts over and over and over. I was prepared for that, it's what I practice, it's how I live, which is why it's what I preach. But the one that surprised me the most, the shift I wasn't quite prepared for, was the shift of feeling my feelings.

I can now confidently report, the shift *Feeling my feelings sets me free!* will not only help you harness your inner awesomeness, it will help heal you and make you whole in a way nothing else can.

It's Okay You Got Distracted

Listen, you glorious raw, unadulterated creature, you're not an idiot. We just don't talk a lot about feeling our feelings—what that means, what that looks like, and tips for how to do it. We're doing it more now than ever before, but as a whole, humans have been very distracted!

Distracted by all the goal setting, all the achieving and accomplishing. Why? Because we forgot! Forgot that we're already as awesome as we need to be by tuning in, accepting what comes up, and picking our focus, bringing it into the present!

We forgot we're not creatures of form, and thought and feelings alone! We forgot that the truth is that we are light, love, energy, one with God. We are expansive, huge, and awesome. We forgot because it's hard to see the unseeable and know the unknowable. But we can wake up! We can wake up to our awesome, remember that our true selves are limitless and that we're being guided and supported!

We got distracted by a certain question, we thought asking it would help us feel better. So we've asked it over and over, like crazy people, thinking the same action would get us a different result. The question:

⊙ WHAT SHOULD I DO?

Or did you say it like this:

⊙ What do I need to do?

⊙ What do you think I should do?

⊙ How do I do that?

⊙ What will I do?

⊙ Do you think I should?

Let the Sound of the "Do" Ring the Alarm!

When you hear yourself ask any of these "do" questions, out loud or in your head, let the punch of the "DO" ring an alarm inside you. That alarm is signifying there's a feeling begging to be felt. An emotion waiting to be examined.

How am I so sure?! Because we humans love to do things instead of feel our feelings.

Doing gets us results. But when you hear the "do" alarm, rejoice! Celebrate! You caught it! You heard it! You're a feelings ninja! And hearing it will answer your question of what to do. When you don't know what to do, it's because you're not sure how you feel.

Projecting and planning are ways of trying to circumnavigate our feelings. If I plan enough, I can avoid pain! If I project and predict this future enough, I can bypass fear!

When we live in the now, when we live in the flow and air hump as we go, we still get lots of things done. We just don't have to force, push, or hustle to do them.

Effort, yes! Work, duh, work is awesome. Shame and force are not needed.

Feeling Your Feelings Will Set You Free

Why did the way my sucky boyfriend looked at me when I became a wild wolf woman while capturing the beanbag hurt so much? Because it hit on an old wound. A wound that told me that feeling my big feelings will disgust the ones I love. I allowed it to enforce an old lie, a lie that I will be alone and rejected if I allow myself to feel or show what I feel. He told me later he hated seeing that side of me. That it was really unattractive to him. As a woman I've been taught that's basically the worst thing ever, to be unattractive, and so it stung so deeply.

What lies about feeling your feelings have followed you? That it's too scary? That it's unsafe? That feeling just makes things worse so you don't want to bother anymore?

By the way, if feeling something has made things worse, you're still in the middle. The feelings are still stuck in you, they haven't been fully felt. Because when they are felt they escape! I'm not saying the memory goes away or all the pain leaves, not always. It's just that the thing that used to cause you so much pain stops driving your life without your consent. Hence, all that freedom!

Maybe it wasn't physically or emotionally safe to feel or show feelings. Maybe you were constantly told, "You're not sad!" or "We don't get angry!"

The first thing to do is determine how you feel about feeling feelings. Ha! But really. You can do this by just noticing your feelings throughout the day without judgment. How do you respond to them? Do you get lost in them? Do you allow having a negative feeling to make you feel like a failure? What do you make feelings mean about you or the people in your life?

This practice invites you to witness and feel your feelings without identifying with them. To notice and observe them. You can feel anger and rage, but they mean nothing about you. You are awesome.

Remember shift number four: *How they feel means nothing about me!* And even how I feel means nothing about me! If it hasn't been physically or emotionally safe to feel your feelings, accepting this idea won't come right away. I practice saying, "It's okay to feel this" when an emotion pops up that I'd usually label as "negative" or "wrong." Or I say, "It's safe to feel whatever I feel."

Feeling your feelings is the opposite of being ruled by them. Feeling your feelings is different from controlling them so you only feel the "right" ones. Feeling your feelings does not mean you have to become some navel-gazing, self-obsessed feelings monitor. And feeling your feelings does not mean you act from all of them.

As I was writing this book, every single time I'd hit a wall, I would not force my way through it. I'd take a break. I'd TAP. If

I found myself planning and projecting, I'd realize I'm not in flow. So I'd lean back and see what feeling I was trying to fight.

You guys. This required so much of me. To feel feelings I've put off feeling my entire life. But holy cow, it's so good. It's hard, but you will feel so FREE. You should maybe be terrified at how free I feel. I know my elderly neighbors who saw me naked in my hot tub on Thanksgiving are.

Feeling your feelings means you feel them. And feeling them will set you free.

Sucky Situations

Everybody wants to know what to do, because we think doing something will make us feel a certain way.

But feelings are confusing. We try to describe the indescribable with thinking and words. Another of many reasons why it's all so confusing is summed up nicely by Dr. Steven Stosny:

> Whatever emotional habit dogs you, it likely has generalized triggers—anything that makes you feel devalued, isolated, or attacked. Over time, the mental states themselves—powerlessness, vulnerability, worthlessness, etc.—trigger habitual responses such as anger, aggression, drinking, overeating, workaholism, independent of the original causes.[11]

In other words, one little feeling can trigger a whole other mental state, which can trigger another response, and that response, well, that can trigger another feeling.

Because it can be so layered and confusing to feel what we feel, we often just feel drained. So then we start to look for things to do to not feel drained. Stimulants, distractions, drugs of all fun shapes and sizes. We drain ourselves more by finding more to do, more to think about, more to dissect, hoping it will all make us feel better.

We take breaks and still feel drained! Go on vacation and need a vacation after our vacation! We do all the prescribed self-care, draw our dream boards, and STILL have zero motivation.

But being a dedicated detective to helping people feel as awesome as they are, I noticed there were three primary situations that seemed to be confusing and tripping people up. These situations were sucking people of their will to feel awesome, and so I very technically labeled them: Sucky Situations.

I've taught these Sucky Situations for years. But in working to feel my feelings, I realized that they are wildly helpful in directing you to identify what exactly is sucking you dry.

Giving these Sucky Situations names helps bring feelings out of the dark and into the light, where you can shine your awesome all over them.

If you hear the alarm of the "do," huzzah! You've noticed there's a feeling to feel. And if you're having a hard time feeling it, you can ask yourself if you might be in the messy middle of, avoiding, or not realizing one of these Sucky Situations.

SUCKY SITUATION #1: Things turned out differently than you thought they would. Losing a child, getting cancer, going through a divorce, losing a job, being betrayed by a friend—one of the reasons it hurts so much is because we simply weren't expecting it.

The shock of the year 2020 is a crazy, universal "things turned out differently than you thought they would."

It all turned out wildly different than we thought it would.

We had made plans and dreams, scheduled vacations and made investments, all based in the reality that this one thing would turn out a certain way. And then it did not. Oh, holy hell, it did not.

Why does this suck? Not just because of the grief, and the loss, and the physical difficulties of something like an illness or divorce. It sucks because it messes with our sense of safety, which is a base and core human need in any human need's psychology model. The need to feel secure and that we can gain pleasure and avoid pain.

It sucks because it toys with us and mocks the illusion of control we all desperately hang on to.

How I feel in Sucky Situation #1 will be different from how you feel. I've been having friends make lists of how they feel in each of the three Sucky Situations. We all have different emotions listed in each column. I invite you to jot down, in your book or elsewhere, what emotions each suck brings up. Honestly the language that you use on a day-to-day basis will speak to you the most.

The power in identification is understanding.[12] It's easier to allow ourselves to feel when we understand why something just plain sucks. No supposed tos, no shoulds, no "I'm ungrateful for feeling this," just: "Oh, I feel fear."

And then you can use TAP to turn back to your awesomeness and flow, baby, flow.

SUCKY SITUATION #2: People were mean. I should warn you that practicing shifts like *How they feel means nothing about me!* and *Feeling my feelings sets me free!* won't keep you immune from getting your feelings hurt. Yes, you choose your freaking focus, and yes, there's no problem to solve, and you'll allow your feelings to be hurt way less. You'll be more resilient and feel more awesome! But if you want to show up and really connect, there will be painful interactions.

Choosing to feel awesome now doesn't mean you won't get bothered, offended, annoyed, or blow up at your kids or mom. It simply invites you to observe all of it from the place of your true self, your awesome.

I used to think that if I showed up to every situation and person in my life with love, lived in the flow, and took only inspired action, that I'd never hurt anyone. That I wouldn't say anything offensive and people would treat me with the love I treated them with. Basically that I'd be beyond reproach. When people or situations turned out differently than I thought they would, it really, really bothered me. And then I was bothered that I was bothered.

But instead of wanting to be a robot yet again, I felt the sadness. I get sad when I can't control the world or force people to love me. And yet the simple act of acknowledging when I feel let down, hurt, sad, or scared can bring so much relief.

We get lost in complicated details of interpersonal relationships. That's why summing up why you're feeling drained in three words is so helpful: *People were mean. Someone was mean. I was hurt.*

Realizing that you're having a hard time feeling awesome, because someone is being mean, sucks. And not acknowledging it is sucking the life out of you. Whether it's hateful comments online, or someone being physically abusive, allowing yourself to feel that pain keeps you in the present and alert to what's happening. In the present moment you can more clearly see how to seek out safety, set boundaries, or speak up for yourself.

How do you feel when someone is mean? Or someone lets

you down? How do you feel when someone belittles or shames you? It's easy to skip over this feeling and go straight into a re-action. Allowing the feeling now means you might not have to keep reliving it later.

SUCKY SITUATION #3: You can't stop beating yourself up.
Maybe you know exactly what is making you feel bad. You even know exactly what you feel. Or so you think; that's why Sucky Situation #3 has been my personal nemesis. Ruminating is a hell I know too well.

"I know what I feel! I felt it! Why can't I stop reliving it and thinking about it? Why can't I let it go?" I've sobbed so many times.

News flash: If you can't stop beating yourself, you're not let-ting yourself feel something. You're either refusing to accept, to allow, or to forgive. Shame is the star of this Sucky Situation. Shame and its BFF, blame.

Shame and blame are a cycle. When you can't handle the shame, when it's too painful to feel, you shift to blame. And round and round it goes.

I called my friend and very talented life coach Jody Moore in a fit of desperation over a sucky interaction with a friend I could not let go. She pointed out my shame/blame cycle. "How do you feel?" she asked.

I started to shame, "I should feel this way, I know I should . . ." and then blame, "But it's like she knows just how to hurt me! It's so mean what she's doing."

So she did what I do to everyone else, put aside my explana-tion, and asked again, "How do you feel?"

I sat down on the sidewalk I had been frantically pacing and started crying. "I'm sad but I already felt that! I gained ten pounds! I ate and cried and stayed in bed! I don't want to be sad anymore!" I sobbed.

"But you're not done being sad. Because you're still sad."

Dammit!

If you're in Sucky Situation #3, and you can't stop beating yourself up, something needs to be felt. You might need a coach, like I did, to help you see it. You might need a therapist, some EMDR therapy, some acupuncture or energy work. You might need medication to help you through the fog. You might just need patience. Patience knowing that trying to rush a feeling is like trying to rush strep throat out of your body. It will pass when it's run its course. We hate accepting this and think that if we practice the tools to feel awesome now, that means we should feel good all the time.

No. Feeling awesome now means you can feel super, super bad, like terrible, awful, barely functioning bad, but still have the awareness that it's not reality. That reality is love and light and expansion. And the darkness is just part of that. Feeling awesome now is knowing both can exist. You can be in pain while hoping for its relief.

If you can't stop beating yourself up, reliving stupid things you said, shuddering with flashbacks to the presentation or confrontation, or if you can't stop telling yourself how worthless and crap you are or someone else is, a feeling is trapped or needs to be felt.

I've noticed feelings surface in layers, showing themselves inch by inch, slower than the most torturous striptease. Every layer needs to be felt. I think our bodies or minds know when we can handle more, or when they can't keep the feeling in any longer, and that's when old memories or feelings can ambush us.

This is another reason 2020 was so painful for so many. We

slowed down and all those feelings we'd been repressing with our constant doing and hustling cackled triumphantly, "Finally! MY TIME TO SHINE!"

Be gentle with yourself always. You're so strong and resilient. You're a beautiful creation being held together by chewing gum and tape. Removing your temporary fixes is uncomfortable. But you can do it. You get to do it! It's a miracle. And it's awesome.

Prevent the Spiral

Using Visualization to Feel Your Feelings

My kids and I are learning how to feel our feelings together. I'm always so impressed with how good they are at it. There are a million ways to feel your feelings. Dancing, writing, shouting, breaking things, crying, listening. Meditation and sitting still.

But one practice I use over and over is visualization. I use this with my kids and myself often.

For ease, I'll just walk you through one like I do with my kids and myself, okay?

Take a deep breath in. And out. Allow yourself to melt, to relax. Notice anywhere in your body that resists. Just notice.

Now in your mind's eye, see yourself in your power, your

awesome, as a ball of light, or standing tall and proud. Maybe you visualize yourself running free or doing something you love. Maybe you see yourself clearly, maybe you have no form. Nothing is right or wrong, just wait until you can visualize yourself as this power and love.

From this place of the powerful witness, lean back. Relax. And observe the feelings that come up.

You can assign them colors, shapes, names, or sounds.

Speak them out loud or in your mind.

You're doing such a good job facing those heavy feelings. Allow yourself to notice where you feel them in your body.

Continue to breathe in, and out.

Allow your powerful self to feel and accept the feelings. Breathing in the feeling with your inhale, and releasing it with your exhale.

I do this with myself and my kids until we feel relief, either in the form of the emotion coming up, or peace.

And then I tell my kids how brave and amazing they are for having so many feelings. For being scared to raise their hand and ask a question, but doing it anyway. How brave they are to walk around and still show up, even when they are confused and uncertain.

They are brave and so are you. We can feel our feelings. Feeling them and allowing them to pass through you will peel back layer after layer of truth about you. Until you hit the core of your essence. That core being that you are exactly perfect, just as you are in whatever you feel. You cannot be too much of yourself, you cannot be too little of yourself. Give yourself the unconditional love you so crave from others, feel what comes up and accept it, it will set you free.

8

I'm Uniquely Qualified to Live My Life!

*When I dare to be powerful—to use my strength
in the service of my vision—then it becomes less
and less important whether I am afraid.*

—AUDRE LORDE

Our neighborhood hosts an annual white elephant gift exchange, and it's always such a good time. I tend to genuinely like the gifts many people have brought in jest, and often go home with something I find useful and delightful. Several years ago my very wonderful neighbor Jane made pillowcases with fabric that featured sexy shirtless illustrations of the Founding Fathers. Baberham Lincoln, if you will. I snatched up Thomas Jefferson and his bulging biceps faster than you can ring the Liberty Bell!

I used the pillowcases during my broken rib recovery to cheer me up, but I kind of lost track of them after that. Just recently I realized that my eight-year-old son, Rad, had been sleeping with a shirtless president pillow for months. It's not that I didn't notice it for several months, I saw the pillow every night as I put him to bed, but it was only recently I realized that it might be kind of funny that that's the pillow my third grader was using. I saw it every night, registered "all is well," and that was that.

Most of the shifts I'm sharing in this book are the result of me beating myself up to learn and accept them, but this one, *I'm uniquely qualified to live my life!*, is one that comes more naturally to me. Maybe it's because I've been saying the mantra "Only you can be you!" for over a decade, but it's also because I have a knack for not seeming to care about a lot of the things other people seem really worried about. Like what kind of pillowcase my son is sleeping with.

The top questions I get, and have gotten my entire online career, stay the same whether I'm hosting dance parties, teaching sugar cookie courses, doing brand consulting, creating podcasts, or just sharing nonsense dancing online. They are: "How do I get more confidence?" And "How do I get more motivation?"

I guess these are the things I seem to portray to the world, as no matter what I'm doing, people think I have endless wells of both.

The shift *I'm uniquely qualified to live my life!* is a wonderful start.

You Don't Need More Motivation

But maybe you're too tired and overwhelmed to live your life, so you're thinking, *Answer that motivation question, Alison!* With my cheerleader-like enthusiasm, and it probably doesn't hurt that I'm a blonde, people are under the illusion that I have boundless energy and therefore all the motivation in the world.

The reality is that I, Alison, do not have boundless energy. But I do know how to get tapped into THE boundless energy. Into the energy that flows through me and you and the trees and the rocks. Yes, the rocks.

Which energy is that? Our AWESOME! The energy that created us all, the energy that unites us all. What Lao Tzu writes about in the twenty-fifth verse of *Tao Te Ching*:

> Something mysteriously formed,
> Born before heaven and earth.
> In the silence and the void,
> Standing alone and unchanging,
> Ever present and in motion.
> Perhaps it is the mother of ten thousand things.
> I do not know its name.
> Call it Tao.
> For lack of a better word, I call it great.[13]

If you want more motivation, or energy, and guidance for living the life that you're uniquely qualified to live, you need to plug in! How? By deciding to TAP into your inner awesomeness. Plug into the "greatness" from which we came. When I tap into that energy, or more accurately let go of the blocks I have to it, well, it feels good. Not only does it feel good for me, it feels good for those who are around me.

Feeling Whole Comes from Inside Yourself

So here's what happens. I get on a stage, or a computer screen, or I write a book, and I bring a taste of this energy to those watching or reading, and momentarily they feel good. They feel a glimpse of this energy, what I keep calling "awesome," and label it as "motivation."

And then I get labeled as a "motivational" speaker. And a good one, because hot damn! At that moment people feel "motivated." But then what usually happens?

After hearing me speak, a beautiful woman named Jennifer said to me, "If I'm being honest, I feel really good right now! But I know I'll wake up tomorrow and feel bad again. What should I do?"

The real root of this issue is this: Jennifer, and all of us, often seek the energy *outside ourselves* to make us feel whole. To make us feel motivated, confident, worthy, or inspired.

So whether from a motivational speaker, a great book, an inspiring person, or something else, you get that hit, that taste of whole boundless great energy, and you start to think that if you "get" more of that, you'll feel good again.

Instead, you wake up the next day, feel like crap again, and think some version of:

This is why you can't trust people! They lie to you!

Or *I knew this wouldn't work for me. My problem is so unique, nothing works for me!*

Or *I'm an idiot. I felt good for a minute but I can't seem to make it work! Why am I so bad at everything?*

When we can't re-create the energy that was displayed to us, we start our search for the next idea, book, cause, or plan that we are sure will make us better, right, or whole. You can see how it's easy to go through life thinking, *Nothing works, nothing can help me feel better.*

And it keeps us busy, and life goes on. But more and more my goal is that the words I say and the feeling I bring will give you a glimpse into your own whole, great energy. That you will realize you don't need anything outside of yourself to feel how great you are. That you will be able to FEEL it and flow from it and tap into it and know you are whole. You are awesome. Exactly as you are. You are uniquely qualified to live your life.

You Are Not a Lazy Loser

When we search for energy, motivation, or confidence outside of ourselves, we just end up putting more things on our plate. It's like my six-year-old, Fiona, who has a completely full plate but shouts, mouth full and frantic, as her siblings are grabbing seconds, "I NEED MORE TOO!" We do this with "shoulds" and "can'ts" and "I don't wanna but I have tos." We pile them heaping on our plates.

"I should work out. I can't eat sugar, I don't wanna go to that dinner but I have to. I should call my mother-in-law, I can't miss that deadline, I don't wanna clean my bathroom but I have to. I should get myself a nicer car, I can't afford it! I don't wanna take that extra side project but I have to!"

The very things we're doing to give us more energy so that we can do more things actually suck us of our energy, and so we add more things! Shoulds, can'ts, and I don't wannas will drain you of the very thing you're searching for: energy. You keep adding goals and to-dos to your list, beating yourself into submission to achieve them, or not keeping them and then feeling like a failure, a lazy loser.

But remember this: You are uniquely qualified to live your life! We need you to live it, and live it well! So let's just get this locked in: You are not a lazy loser.

You are overwhelmed, you are exhausted, you probably have a lot of feelings you don't want to feel, or can't feel, and they are draining you. You have worries and concerns, and you're beating the crap out of yourself to do better, make your body better, your life better, and the world better.

Cut yourself some slack. You are freaking awesome.

You are the only person on this planet who gets to live your life. How could it be possible that you are not qualified, equipped, good enough, or worthy to live it? IT IS NOT POSSIBLE. It doesn't even make sense!

You have the exact skills you need to live your life.

You have all the time you need to do the things that need doing.

If you feel called to do it, freaking do it.

People with Clean Cars Clean Their Cars

Like a lot of creative people, I can have a very difficult time with organization. I used to be constantly overwhelmed with a messy house and no clean laundry. But like the sexy president pillowcase, I could ignore it all for months, only to wake up one day and be horrified at the chaos. But as my children got older, and I brought more people into my business, they all seemed to need more order. And, honestly, I did too.

Then one day it dawned on me: people with clean cars, they clean out their cars! I kid you not, this was a revolutionary thought to me.

So I started doing this thing, where every time I get out of the car, I clean out whatever is in it. I know, I AM WILD! And lo and behold, I am now a person with a clean car, because, you guessed it, I clean my car! This gave me more energy and made one part of my life easier. I had more capacity. I wanted to do this more places in my life.

So as I continued to build my business and my team, I decided what I was terrible at was building systems. Learning that cleaning my car when I get out is a system, I decided I could make more. So I got obsessed with that, that I had to be like those business babes who build all those email systems, and content systems, and funnels, and track their analytics. I hired other people to make systems, and I talked to people who are very good at systems. I needed systems for working out, eating healthy, and meditating! Give me all the systems!

And guess what happened?

My work, which has always flowed and been inspired, started to make me miserable. The systems made me sad and rebellious against myself. I didn't want to exercise, I wanted to watch the entire *Vampire Diaries* series all the way through for the fifth time, because I was drained and felt no motivation or energy.

I had piled all those shoulds and can'ts and I don't wannas but I have tos so high on my plate, it was too heavy to carry.

And I stopped believing that I was uniquely qualified to live my life and run my business. I started believing I had to do it the same way all those better, healthier, more successful people did. That's when I got the closest to quitting everything than I'd ever been before.

Inspired Order Creates Capacity

So is the moral of the story we should just give up and live messy, chaotic lives? Maybe! But probably not. I'd like to report that I am very happy with my business, my car is clean, and my house is mostly picked up. I'm not trying to brag but I even ate vegetables yesterday, well, maybe not yesterday, but for sure the day before.

The moral of the story is that, yes, order creates capacity, and having systems in place will enable you to more easily feel awesome, but that order must be inspired by you! You are uniquely qualified to live your life, to create the systems you need to help you do it, and to adjust and change them as your life grows and evolves.

In the hugely popular *Women Who Run with the Wolves* by Clarissa Pinkola Estés, which you should totally read, she shares one of my favorite exercises for learning to listen to your instinct and inner wisdom. To me it is the perfect example of how to build inspired systems that tap you into boundless energy and help you create more capacity for living your life!

Here's the general idea.

Imagine a giant banquet table covered with the most wonderful, delicately prepared food. You can have anything you like on the table! There's so much to choose from, and all of it looks delicious, so you start loading your plate.

Okay, pause. This right here is how we approach our schedules. We look at a table that has a lot of wonderful selections and begin to load our plate. The table might be piled high with ideas we see on social media, or the news, or a bunch of how-to books, or what our society or upbringing has laid forth as acceptable and good. In my case I felt like I had to fill my plate with the same shiny systems as all the other successful women I know have.

But then you're standing there, with a dish piled high with delicious foods, and realize this isn't what you really wanted. So you put down the plate. And you clear the table. And you realize you're hungry for, as Estés says, some celery with peanut butter. But that was not on the table!

How do we live in the flow, tap into that great boundless energy, and follow our inner knowing? Start with a clear table. The decision to feel awesome constantly invites you back to a clear table. The table of reality and truth, the reality that you are greatness, and an infinite creator.

The old idiom "We greatly overestimate what we can do in a day or a year, and greatly underestimate what we can do in a lifetime" holds so much wisdom.

Like Alcoholics Anonymous wisely teaches, the way to create, live, and feel the life of your dreams is to do it one day at a time.

Inspired order creates capacity, so let's do it one day at a time, connected to your inner knowing, with the confidence it's guiding you to your truest, most glorious truth and life, to your awesome.

What Do You Want Your Days to Look Like?

When I coach people on building their dream life and business and doing what they feel called to do, I always ask, "What do you want your days to look like? What do you want them to feel like?"

The reason for this is because I'm not going to spend time helping you figure out how to tap into your motivation to run a marathon if your ideal day does not include running. Starting on this micro level, with a clear table, is a beautiful exercise to help you do that.

Recently I was working with two sisters I adore, Chanté and Alexis, and I asked them this question. They are doing insanely important work in unity and diversity education. It's work they feel called to, work that inspires and drives them.

Their social media and speaking opportunities were blowing up! But they felt frantic and tired with all the demands on their time, the never-ending cycle of social media content creation, and how to balance it all with their cumulative six children, other jobs, and busy life! They were very overwhelmed.

So before we made any business plans for service offers, future events, or what to post online, I asked, "What do you want your days to look like?"

The sweet, overworked sisters responded by relaying what their days currently looked like, and all the ways they were falling short. They told me about jam-packed schedules. "I want to have inspirational activities for my kids, and healthy meals, and get a workout in, and get enough sleep, and be there for my husband, his job is exhausting!" Alexis told me. "I want to do this all but then I find myself just so tired, I'm just mindlessly scrolling social media! That's the problem! I need to stop doing that!" Alexis said.

"We try to get together at night after bedtime to work on Let's Talk Sis, but our kids won't stay in bed, or we can't focus hard enough!" said Chanté.

Like so many of us, Alexis and Chanté were so deep in the spiral of shoulds, can'ts, and the ever-draining "I know what to do, I'm just not doing it" that they couldn't imagine a reality where they got to choose what their days looked like. They couldn't clear the table.

What I'm asking you to do is remember this is your life. You are uniquely qualified to live it. Which also means you can let go of anything you want. Chanté and Alexis were expecting so much of themselves, they were losing themselves.

Like I started saying to myself when I was having a panic attack about going on a service mission for my church, *I'm an adult and I can do whatever the hell I want!* I canceled the mission and stopped believing in God or anything else for a while instead.

See! You're an adult and you can do whatever you want. There will be consequences, and of course your choices affect others, but one of the reasons you're so drained and in so much need of motivation is because you're not living your life as you. You're living life as the person you think you're supposed to be. This is SO EXHAUSTING.

Listen, lover, your best looks different every single day. Lots of days I come home from work and Eric asks, "How was it?" I tell him, "It was a shitty best day, my best was pretty shitty, but I did it!"

Or as Mother RuPaul says, "And if I fly or if I fall, at least I can say I gave it all."

Our expectations of ourselves determine what and who we surround ourselves with, our expectations determine what we put on our to-do lists and calendars. And those things can run our life, and constantly drain us if we let them.

But when what surrounds you reflects what you value, you will not be drained. Let me say that one more time for the people in the back! When what surrounds you reflects what you value, it won't drain you!

That's how you get more motivation, and motivation leads to confidence.

The trick here is knowing what you value.

I used to value everything, and so I valued nothing. I cared so much about every single thing because I thought caring meant controlling, and it drained me.

Control is not what my soul, my spirit, my divine creator self values. Control is rooted in fear and lack! And so I was drained.

Your body will rebel against you not living authentically. I wasn't meant to go on that mission but I was forcing it, and my body rebelled.

When you shift your value to feel awesome now, excess expectations fall away. You design your days with inspired systems that reflect your personality.

Prevent the Spiral

Tools You Can Use Now

Take an inventory of expectations. If you ask yourself *What do I want my days to look like?* and you feel overwhelmed with shoulds, remember this: you are not a free unlimited resource. It's time to take a look at your expectations. How much do you expect yourself to do every single day? Are you expecting it because other people are? Because it's what you used to do?

One of my friends and business expert Susan Petersen always says, "Systems break with speed and velocity." Just because a system, or how much you get done in a day, used to serve you, it doesn't mean it always will. When my life speeds up or grows, the systems that used to serve me break. That's when I need to accept more help or slow down in other areas.

I asked the sisters, "If I told you that you could have four hours every week, just to breathe and think about your business, Let's Talk Sis, how does that feel?"

They both let out a huge sigh of relief. With the table clear, with endless possibilities, they saw a possible solution that their inner knowing confirmed as correct with peace and a sense of joy. I promised them if they would commit to themselves and pay for childcare, not bring in more work for themselves by trading for it, that within thirty days we'd have a plan in place to pay for it easily. They did this, and they, of course, didn't even end up needing me to make a plan to bring that money in. They are geniuses at what they do! As soon as they had the space carved out, everything they needed flowed in. Also, you should hire them to speak!

So let's pause here and I'll ask you the same question. Take a quick inventory. If you could have four hours every week to dedicate solely to the thing that makes you feel a sense of purpose, how would that make you feel?

Now that the table is clear, what would it take to get those four hours on your schedule? Like Chanté and Alexis, do you need to find someone to watch your kids or clean your house? Do you need a dedicated space to focus on the work? Something else? Be specific about what those things are and then you can start allowing the solutions to present themselves.

Manage your transitions. Starting with a clear table is especially important during transitions, which is when I am moving from one activity to the next. There's quantitative and qualitative proof that successful people manage transitions well, but I'm more interested in what happy, content people do these days. And managing my transitions keeps me mindful, plugged in, and flowing.

Start every day, every meeting, every hour that you can, and each new task with a clear table. Ask yourself what's the focus, what's your intention? Allow the past to stay in the past and the future to stay in the future, focusing on the now.

As I transition from activity to activity I remind myself to TAP. For example, here's what my TAP process looks like before I go to teach:

TUNE IN: How do I feel in that moment, tired, excited, anxious? I allow my feelings to reveal my true intentions. When I feel scared or anxious, I'm probably trying to control how others perceive me. When I feel rushed, I'm feeling a lack of time.

ACCEPT: Okay, I'm more worried about looking good during this teaching time than serving. I accept that. I'm a little more tired today, I accept that.

PICK MY FOCUS: My true intention is service. My true intention is love. I choose to focus on speaking to hearts, not minds. I choose to focus on knowing I have all the time and energy I need, to live this moment.

And boom! I show up feeling more awesome and less drained. More focused on flow and service than on how I look.

Make it a fun experiment. I now treat all my projects, systems, and schedule like an experiment. Inspired order does expand capacity. But I can't know if a system serves me until I try it. So when creating a new system or schedule for myself, such as a plan for getting more vegetables in my diet, or more quality time with my kids, I create it from a place of flow, not force. I believe it can feel fun and easy. And if it doesn't work, well, then

I'm on my way! I can try something different next week and see if that works.

I've used this same principle to build a business for myself that includes day-to-day work with mostly things that feel effortless for me. I learned that recording my podcast feels wonderful, so I shifted my products and work to more speaking and recording. It works for now. My days are full of flow. And if it stops working, I can always try something else. No sweat.

Here's How This Makes the World Better

Why does it matter that you believe that you are uniquely qualified to live your life not just so you can get more done, not just so you can feel less crappy because you're checking things off your list? It matters because expanding capacity increases compassion.

I often look back at my life and think, *How did I miss that? That person's suffering? That tragic world event? How did I miss this prejudice in my perspective?* And then I stop and realize it's because I was so filled and fueled with self-loathing, frantic action, and anxiety, that I had much less capacity and space to hold for other people's suffering.

When people approach me and want to have a difficult conversation, I don't feel so overwhelmed and so drained that I can't hear a different perspective anymore. I really believe in my core that people want to make a difference, that people want to understand, that people want to connect. But I also believe that so many of us are carrying so much suffering and so much pain and so much overwhelm and so much anxiety that we are unable to hear and listen to other people because we are so bogged down ourselves.

You are not a lazy loser. You don't need more energy. You don't need more motivation. You simply need to align your life to your intentions. Because you are uniquely qualified to live your life!

When you align with what lights you up, what expands you, when you follow what makes you feel joy and ease and peace, your energy increases. Your capacity and productivity increase. Your compassion for other people increases. But it all grows in a sustainable way fueled by purpose.

When you can feel and enjoy every part of the process of your life, the result holds less weight. You won't miss your beautiful life believing that you don't have what it takes to live it. And there's no greater result than being able to enjoy the beautiful life you've created.

9

There's No Problem to Solve!

> No problem can be solved from the same consciousness that created it.
>
> **—ALBERT EINSTEIN**

I was born smack-dab in the middle of five kids, and all of us are pretty close in age. And in case you were wondering, yes, each and every one of them is as nuts as I am with just as much to say as I do! The Faulkner clan goes: Kirk, Evan, Alison, Andrea, and Blake, who is the caboose baby golden child. But my mom had the first four of us in the span of six years. So my brother Evan is just a few years older, and he was the perfect age for all my high school friends to be in love with. He and his hunky friend Jesse were often the reason my house was the place to hang.

Evan and Jesse, like many teenage boys in the late 1990s and early 2000s, were often quoting Adam Sandler movies. And their favorite line to recite, in response to just about anything, was, "Don't tell me my business, devil woman!"

Just in case you can't quickly reference *Billy Madison*, here's the scene it comes from.

Wealthy and wild idol Billy Madison (Adam Sandler) is playing a prank with some friends on an innocent-enough-seeming old man. They scrape some dog poop off the sidewalk and put it in a brown paper bag. They then drop the bag on the old man's farmhouse doorstep.

Right before they ring the doorbell they light the bag on fire, and then of course run away to watch the scene unfold from the bushes.

In true Adam Sandler style, the quirkiest old man ever comes to the door in his underwear and, horrified, shouts to his off-screen wife, "Judas priest, Barbara! It's one of those flaming bags again!"

She shouts back, "Don't put it out with your boots, Ted!" To which he yells, "Don't tell me my business, devil woman!"

Ted, of course, wearing hiking boots with his tighty-whities, stomps out the fire, smells his boots, and then wails, "It's poop again!"

Naturally, Billy Madison and his other adult male friends playing this adolescent prank are beside themselves with laughter. But enter now, my point:

Problems are exactly like flaming bags of poop.

The sooner you can identify problems for what they are, the easier it is to discover that there's no problem to solve, which will help you access your awesomeness.

What's Your Problem?

I want to make sure you don't misunderstand and think I'm telling you there's nothing wrong with your life or the world. That we should dismiss your suffering, your pain, your health issues, your safety concerns. That those bills piling up don't need to be paid. Absolutely not. But the commitment I made, the one I believe in, and the intention I've invited you to, is to be able to feel awesome now! As in, now! Even with these issues and concerns. Even in the imperfection. In the only moment we have, the only moment we ever had, the only place we truly ever are: the now.

So often we spend our time projecting and planning to get ahead of potential problems. We create an entire life centered around avoiding problems only to be shocked and offended when all our micromanaging couldn't prevent a world pandemic.

We listen, and treat as truth, the created stories of our wandering, unconscious mind. Stories filled with one-sided perceptions and the murky fog of our past experience clouding any present clarity.

I'm not saying there are no problems in this world, I'm just inviting you to reframe how you see your present reality.

The Problems We Create

Recently I saw a group of friends I hadn't seen in months through the window of my office. They were chatting on the sidewalk. I ran outside, so thrilled to see them! My level of enthusiasm far outshined theirs. I noticed and thought, *I refuse to accept that problem.* And went on to ask them how they were doing. They answered individually and quickly with, "Good!" And then stood in silence. Determined not to feel bad, I said, "So glad to hear it! What are you doing next!?"

One hesitantly said, "We're going to lunch."

Another shakily offered, "Do you want to go?"

"Thank you, that's okay," I said, "I need to get back to work, but have fun!" And I meant it.

But as a grown-ass lady I still had that high school feeling of, *Do my friends even like me?*

Now, it's no secret by now that I've always been concerned about what people think about me, as I've explored in earlier chapters. The thing is, I used to turn people's reactions to me into a problem to solve. *Why don't they like me? What do I need to change? Like, I think I'm a nice person but maybe I'm not? How can I be a better friend?* What's more, I used to think this made me a really "good," thoughtful person. But all it actually did was make me a really anxious person.

So when I was back inside my office, I took a breath. And I decided to TAP it out. I said to myself, *There's no problem to solve.*

> **TUNE IN:** I tuned in and felt a little sad. I was really excited to see them, they didn't seem excited to see me. Sad.

> **ACCEPT:** I accepted that sad moment, and I did not try to fix it, because sad isn't a problem. It's a feeling. I felt it.
>
> Things I used to do that I did not: I didn't decide what to do when I saw those friends next, I didn't worry about how I should "act." I didn't call my other friends and tell them the story so they could affirm I'm a good friend. I didn't get on social media to avoid the feeling.

PICK YOUR FOCUS: Love. I simply decided: they're not really a bubbly group of gals. That's pretty much their normal, and I love them and wish them the best. I didn't perform love, I didn't force love. I've decided that people get to be them and I'll love them anyway. I've practiced for years and know I still have a lifetime of practice ahead of me.

A few days later I saw the friend who had seemed the least excited to see me. She made eye contact with me! She addressed me! And I said excitedly, "Oh good, I was worried that you didn't like talking to me anymore!" I said it playfully with love, but not defensively. I hadn't planned it, or rehearsed it.

She looked confused for a moment and said, "Oh! The other day. Oh yeah, I was in a really weird headspace. I'm so sorry."

Did I have to say something to her? Did I need to say something? Apparently I did, because I said it! I love this friend and by saying something I gave us the chance to move the friendship forward without resentment.

But what if my friends do hate me? What if they had been talking about me and decided that they really didn't want to be my friend?

Those are things I absolutely cannot control. They get to choose how to feel about me. My friend, the incredible life coach Jody Moore, says, "Give people permission to be wrong about you." Boom, right?!

I cannot control how they feel about me. There's no problem to solve. I can only examine how I feel about myself, and my friends. Trying to decide how I will "act" when I see my friends next takes me out of the present moment and into problem-solving mode.

Problem-Solving Mode Is Not Flow

Think about how you behave in problem-solving mode. For me it's a very narrow focus, very myopic with a sense of urgency. Perhaps I act much like a frantic person trying to put out a fire?

What serves me better is to drop my ego, drop my defensiveness, and try to uncover what I truly feel. I then can determine from a place of awareness: Am I safe, or not safe?

There are relationships in which you are not safe. And what happens in problem-solving mode is we can bypass these important, urgent warnings from our highest self, our awareness. This is always destructive, if not also downright dangerous.

Seth Godin, best-selling author and educator, sends out wonderful quick daily emails. This is one of my recent favorites:

> *Qarrtsiluni*: This is the Inuit word for "sitting together in the darkness, quietly, waiting for something creative or important to occur."
>
> Of course, this works.
>
> The only difficult part is doing it. We're buzzy people, inundated with noise, using it to hide from the important work that's right in front of us.[14]

Getting lost in a problem keeps you from the "important work that's right in front of us." Like realizing if you are unsafe.

In the case of these friends, I am safe. I no longer keep relationships in which I am not. So I openly share love, period. That's my decision. But to share that authentically I have to feel it authentically.

In his wonderful book *The Way of Effortless Mindfulness*,[15] Loch Kelly teaches:

When you shift out of this cloud of emotional or small mind and discover this spaciousness of still, quiet, alert awareness, it's a great relief. You can realize that you are the sky, and the cloudy emotions and thoughts are ever changing weather.

In other words, we can spend so much energy focusing on our problem, the storm in our cloud, that we forget there's a whole sky of awesomeness out there. And the absolute best and most efficient use of our focus is stepping out of our cloud into the vastness of the sky! The sky is full of solutions! When we are tapped into our awesome, which is like the sky, we can take the needed action or nonaction from a place of flow and clarity.

What Do You Let Your Problems Mean About You?

Let's examine how this shift of *There's no problem to solve* makes you feel. Either how it made you feel initially, as hopefully you've warmed up to it, or even right this minute. Obviously we will all feel differently, but as I've talked to many people about it, here are some of their initial reactions to this shift. They feel: attacked, dismissed, defensive, panicked, out of control, lazy, selfish, relieved, confused, exempt, curious, hopeful, angry, or just in some way bothered.

Absolutely no feeling or response is better than any other. In fact, if you're having a hard time with the shift or don't like it, that's fine too! Just give yourself permission to explore it. The reason I ask how you feel when you hear it is because how you feel about it will reveal to you how you attach to, or identify with, problems.

The need to know "I matter and I'm valued" is a core human need, one of the spirit, the soul, our nature, but we don't need to hear it from external sources when we're connected to our awesome. It's ingrained in that level of consciousness. The idea of being "special" or "better than," the desire to feel different, unique, or powerful, in a way that requires us to rank and quantify ourselves and others, is driven by the ego.

I love Dr. Nicole LePera's definition of ego: "Our ego is the identity of ourselves that lives within your mind . . . Ego is not good or bad, it's a neutral part of our psyche that helps us make sense of who we are. Our ego causes us issues when we have unresolved trauma and become attached to the false, negative self-image of ourselves we inherited."[16]

The commitment to feeling awesome is continually inviting us out of our ego, our inevitable false negative self-images that we've created within our mind. It invites us to look outside of ego and into our higher, expanded consciousness that we can access when we sit in the seat of the witness, in presence.

Our ego needs to believe that we are special, that we are better . . . better than who? It depends on our experiences, but mostly, just better than someone else.

How Does This Problem Serve Me?

Over and over again I see myself, and the people at my workshops, spin stories about ourselves and our problems and how unsolvable and impossible they are.

Now, I have a firm belief that humans are not idiots; we aren't doing this because we love being miserable. Which is why it's always so good to ask, *How is this serving me? Why am I so tempted, over and over again to step on the flaming bags of poop?*

Because we all do it! We spin these stories, we live in them and fiddle with them, because doing so gives our ego a false sense of control, and a little boost that our problems, awful as they may be, are our identity, and that makes us feel special and known. Me thinking my friends must not like me is a recurring theme song, one I've been singing since puberty.

We repeat behaviors we believe will benefit us, and by repeating them, they become a habit. So why do we think having problems might benefit us?

Maybe you've gotten a lot of attention for your problems. Maybe when you have a problem, you realize you get a lot of care from your partner. Maybe when you have a problem, your partner leaves you alone and then you get to feel bad. And that's actually maybe a feeling you're more comfortable with than feeling loved and supported and taken care of. Maybe having a problem gives you something to do! Maybe having a problem is just a safety zone that you're used to. And you're so used to being in problem-solving mode that when you're not in that mode, you kind of feel lost and you don't feel like you're yourself.

Maybe having a problem makes you feel important and busy because you're figuring something out, you're working on something. You have a sense of purpose.

This is why I often lovingly say, "The bad news is your problems do not make you a special unicorn! There is a solution for you! The good news is that you are still, in fact, a special unicorn; it's just that everyone else is too!"

Refuse to Accept the Flaming Bags of Poop

Problems, for a lot of us, bring up so much urgency, panic, and a refusal to see from a broader perspective because they make us feel a sense of lack. Lack of time, lack of resources, lack of self-acceptance or belief in your own ability. The problems feel so necessary, so absolutely urgent.

This is why my favorite visual representation of problems is a flaming bag of poop. Because Ted does what we all usually do when we see a problem: he stomps it out with his boots. Even though his wife tells him not to, even though it's clear this isn't the first time the flaming bag he's stepped on has poop in it, he does it anyway.

Like Ted, we're all shocked when we're left with poop on our boots!

Not only do we create, encounter, and find plenty of problems all on our own, but like this scene in *Billy Madison*, people are continually leaving their problems on the front steps of our life.

This might look like when people trash-talk someone and want our outrage and allegiance, when they feel frantic and anxious and don't want to be alone in the feeling. They solicit our anxiety with fear and pressure, on social media, in our in-boxes, in our text messages, in our ears.

If any of you have small children you try to take to school in the morning, you might have ten flaming bags of poop thrown at you before breakfast! "WHERE ARE MY SHOES?! WHERE IS MY JACKET?! I DON'T HAVE A LUNCH!" Why on God's green earth can they never find their own freaking shoes?! Does it ever get better?

And while it's obviously stressful to accumulate all these problems, we still do it!

I'm not suggesting you become a judgmental jerk about problems and walk around smugly sharing with other people, "Ah yes, I see the flaming bag of poop you are directing toward me, and I choose to decline. Good luck with that."

I mean, with some problems, you can absolutely do this. The old man in the truck screaming profanities at me because I didn't pull up in a line fast enough. Yes, his problem gets ignored. Request denied! Even my kids trying to freak me out with their lost shoes, I ignore those problems too. My kids wear some pretty insane things on their feet sometimes.

But what I'm suggesting is that you stay in the seat of the soul, in awareness, and if you're invited to engage, you can see the problem for what it is. An opportunity for a solution, a solution that might have nothing to do with the fire in front of you. From your awesome you might see that there's not a problem, there's really:

- A hurt person who needs love, compassion, or understanding

- A child who needs reassurance

- A frustrated person who needs to be heard

- An opportunity that needs quiet and stillness so it can be discovered

- A solution waiting just outside the narrow focus of the problem

- A moment for gratitude, to show you there's no lack

☉ Or often, as in my case with thinking my friends hate me, that there's truly no problem to be solved

My Body Is Not a Problem to Be Solved

I don't remember a time when my body did not feel like a problem.

I was sitting on the floor during story time in the library when I first noticed it, what a problem my body was. My thighs were bigger and lumpier sitting crisscross applesauce than any of the other girls. *Why are my leg bumps so much bigger?* I thought. I was horrified.

I went on my first diet when I was ten. A frozen-meal weight-loss system. I remember meeting with a consultant, choosing my meals for the week; the blueberry French toast was my favorite. I remember the women in their forties and fifties applauding me at the weekly support group when I said I had turned down birthday cake that week at school.

My weight was not keeping me from living a "normal" life. I was simply bigger. Bigger than the other girls my age. Rounder, louder, larger.

My family believed they were keeping me from being teased and making sure I got asked to the dances. We've come so far in the past thirty years to call out diet culture. They couldn't see that's what this was. They believed the lie that being fat was the worst thing a girl could be. They were also wonderful, supportive people and they loved me. I am what I am because of them.

They just couldn't see that my body had been commodified, that thinness had been commodified. Being fat was a problem; it felt like the only way to see it.

When I was thirteen a nutritionist I'd met with to put me on another diet told my mom after meeting me, "You won't have to worry about that one, she's not the type to get an eating disorder."

I was superoffended. Who was she to limit me?! But she was right, I never had a full-blown eating disorder, just a lifetime of disordered eating. A lifetime of diet after diet, a lifetime of counting calories and making any weight gain an immediate problem that needed to be solved.

Before being hit by a car, I had been counting calories for about a year. I was down to what I almost weighed at my wedding, the ultimate "goal" after having three kids. To be fair, another reason I lost weight is because I felt better. I wasn't living in constant anxiety, and though I was counting calories I wasn't doing it with shame or any sort of intensity that made me ill. I mean other than the three times I got strep throat that year. Oh brother.

After I was hit, I continued counting calories. Even though I couldn't exercise for a while. I allowed my body to have what it needed and told it I loved it. I meant it. For a year I was SO PROUD to not have gained weight after being hit! *See! I lost weight the "right" way! It stayed off!*

I made it mean I was legit! Not a fraud! A successful Zen goddess!

And then my PTSD caught up with me, I sunk into a depression and gained back close to half of what I'd lost. I watched myself with curiosity.

Everyone will know you're a failure, the inner mean girl hissed.

I had no idea that I had equated my body with being a success. I watched it. I stopped counting calories. I didn't try to lose the weight I gained back. I started a new exercise routine and got really strong. I loved it! I could lift heavy things! I met with one of the trainers, only because it was part of the sign-up system. She weighed me and told me how many calories to eat, to see "results." I looked at her lovingly and said, "No, thank you. I'm good. I'm good like this."

She didn't know what to do. I don't think anyone had ever told her they liked their body just how it was.

I bought bigger clothes and practiced saying, "There are so many types of beautiful!" when I walked by the mirror.

I chanted the mantra of my friends at Beauty Redefined, Lexie and Lindsay Kite, and said, "My body is an instrument, not an ornament!" And I felt so good! Another year and a half passed. That weight was okay. I was okay.

And then within two weeks everything changed. COVID-19 hit and I couldn't go to my gym class. I was beyond devastated that I had to downsize my business, which included my friend of fifteen years who had been working with me. I couldn't get out of bed. I felt too much shame, too much sadness.

I hid my scale, deciding there was too much going on to add checking my weight to the list of things to freak out about.

After a few months, I didn't know how my body looked. I didn't know because I couldn't weigh myself. Think about that. I'd look in the mirror and not know how to feel about my body because I didn't have a number to approve or not approve. This showed me even more clearly how much value I'd placed on controlling that number.

But when my pants stopped fitting, it became increasingly obvious. Like a lot of other people in 2020 I'd gained a chunk of weight. Basically the rest of the weight that I'd lost, plus more for good measure. I refer to it as "The Year My Underwear Kept Getting Bigger."

The crazy part is how far I'd come. I'd look in the mirror with love and compassion and say, "These lumps are great! I love this different type of beauty! I love being a luscious woman! I'm healthy! I can serve!" And then I'd see older, thinner pictures of myself and start singing "Memory" from *Cats*: "Life was beautiful then. I remember the time I knew what happiness was . . ." and slump back into discouragement.

I volleyed like this for a while. But the urge to make my weight a problem weighed me down.

Then I started to do something I never thought I would. I started to nitpick and nag my perfect ten-year-old about what she was eating. "You've had too many!" I'd shout. "Put that back!" I'd snap with more intensity than intended.

I caught myself doing it one day and recoiled in horror. That pain of knowing everyone was watching everything I was eating, that pain of feeling like losing weight made the people I loved love me more, and gaining weight made them love me less—was I going to pass that pain on to her?

I doubled down on my decision to refuse to make my body, or *any* body, a problem to be solved. There was no problem to solve. There was a person who needed to heal.

When I barked at my beautiful innocent Ginger, it was like I was shouting at my ten-year-old self. I didn't realize how much I was disgusted with the little girl I used to be. So I started working to heal that. I hung a picture of me at age eight, when I was just starting to fill out to the concern of those around me, in my boudoir, a tiny room I've taken over in my house that's basically a closet.

I'd look at the photo of me in my "Under the Sea" dance recital costume, proudly holding maracas, and as I got dressed for the day I'd blow the photo a kiss. Sometimes I'd look at it and just say, "You were trying so hard. I'm so proud of you."

I don't give any craps if anyone thinks this is cheesy. I'd do anything not to pass my pain to my kids. Anything. I felt guided and directed to do this, so I did it. And after a while, I stopped noticing what Ginger was eating. I stopped trying to control her.

But it has not been that easy to stop trying to attack myself.

I wrote this to myself one night to let out the sadness:

> The urge that my weight is a problem to be fixed, a "problem" that should be given priority and trump all other projects and focus until "corrected," is so deep in me I almost don't know what to do with it. Like every logical piece of me knows it's not a problem. But my urge to fix it—as if it was—it's more real than I ever realized. It's hard to sit with. I feel like an addict going through withdrawals.
>
> And as I sit with the urge, and refrain from trying to fix it for the first time in my life, it starts to play games with me and trick me. Trick me into believing that I am THIS problem to be fixed. I am the problem.
>
> And then I see why that urge to fix the "problem" is so, so deep. Because if I'm the problem, and I will be less valued because I am this problem, fixing it becomes a matter of life or death. Being accepted, being praised, being liked, my weight, my size, my person, my body—which quickly becomes me as a whole, though I know it is not, becomes the problem.

I have to fix it or die. Fix it or be alone. Even though that reality is not playing out by anyone but me. Even though I know it's a lie.

You want to hear that I stopped making my body a problem, and now I'm the weight I've always dreamed of being, right? That all my old pants fit again, and the weight effortlessly melted off? It's not true. That's not what happened. This mindset is us still trying to fix something that's not a problem.

And I'm still in the middle of the experiment!

But what I can tell you is this. I get up, and I don't obsess over my body every waking minute. I get up, I put on my bigger pants and I stop thinking about it. I get up and I'm grateful if I'm healthy enough to do what I need and want to do. I'm not blinded by the desire to look different while I do it.

I look in the mirror or at a photo sometimes and feel a bit sad. I accept that sadness and I don't shame myself for it. I feel it. And then I forget about it, usually for a day or two at a time.

After thirty-plus years of thinking about it nonstop, I'd say that's pretty good. I feel sexy with my husband and confidently wear whatever I've decided I like, regardless of if it's "flattering."

I turn myself on, I love my body! But I also often feel fairly neutral toward it—and still occasionally, disgust. I thank God to be lucky enough to see that my body is not a problem to be solved.

Prevent the Spiral

Problem-Flipping Tools

Seeing our circumstances as a problem is a decision. For me, making the decision *not* to see it as a problem is a decision that makes me feel better, less drained, and more resilient. Here are some of my favorite quick problem-flipping tools:

Use this mantra: "This moment is the perfect teacher." This mantra invites you into the present moment to see solutions. And ask "What does this moment invite me to learn?" when you start to slip into problem-solving mode.

Express gratitude. This redirects your focus. Some examples of mantras to express gratitude: I'm grateful for solutions. I'm grateful for opportunities. I'm grateful I can feel energized. I'm grateful I can feel inspired. I'm grateful I'm powerful. I'm grateful I am light. I'm grateful I can do great things with ease. I'm grateful solutions are on their way.

Move your body. The fastest way to shift your mood is to move your body. You don't have to think about this just as exercise! Dance, jump, wiggle, walk to the other side of the room, it's the fastest way to shift your mindset. Move your body or lose your mind!

When in doubt, TAP it out. Tune in with journaling, meditation, or quiet. Accept what comes up. Feel what you can. Pick your focus, the present moment; in this moment, you have enough. There's no problem to solve. Take any inspired action or nonaction that arises.

I Am Not a Problem

If you identify with your problems, you become the problem. This too easily translates in our minds to *I am a problem, and here's what I need to fix.* Even if you have some problems, which now I hope we can all see is just a label we assign, *you* are not a problem.

You don't need to be fixed or solved or changed. You get to be you. Just as you are. And who are you? You're a creator! You are awareness, love, light, expansion, energy, God.

Believing this won't keep you from taking action and evolving. It will keep you creative and resilient. Pick what expands your soul, not what calls you into the deep dark hole. Run, walk, dance, or slowly crawl toward the light. Take all the breaks you need. Dodge every bag of flaming dog poop you possibly can.

10

I Get to Show Up
as I Am, Right Now!

I never rehearse to be myself.

—WALTER MERCADO

I've always loved talking, I'm just so thrilled when anyone seems interested in listening! But my voice has forever been low and scratchy and gets strained easily. Growing up in Southern California, it started to be an issue in high school during Santa Ana season—peaking in October, when the winds blow hard and the air is especially dry. I'd go to answer a question in school and not be able to get out much sound. Whispering and croaking like a frog during the morning periods of the day. After a few seasons of this, at age fifteen I was taken to an ear, nose, and throat doctor.

After examining me, he explained that I had simply learned

to speak incorrectly. I draw air and sound from my throat rather than my diaphragm, and doing so puts a lot of tension on my vocal cords. This had given me the beginning of vocal nodules, which he said would most likely just get worse. He instructed, "You can do some speech therapy, but overall this won't be too much of a problem in your life. Just don't go into a career where you use your voice a lot, you know, like teaching or public speaking."

I'll never forget the true out-of-body experience I had when he said that. I had this mental image flash before my eyes of a woman, full of enthusiasm and power, speaking on a black stage, shrouded in darkness except for the light around her. I couldn't see the audience, but I knew they were there. A blue velvet curtain hanging behind the scene; I just vividly remember the rich sapphire blue of those curtains! And I knew, with complete certainty, that woman was me.

I remember laughing when the doctor told me that, seeing in what was probably only one or two seconds that vision. I told him, "Ha! That's probably exactly what I'll do."

The image is one that has come back to me throughout my life, but only after the fact can I see what a guiding gift it is. Because mostly what it used to do was make me feel insane. I was too embarrassed to talk to or ask anyone about it, because what was I saying? That I was going to be a superstar? No one, not in my world at least, was having talks about visions you might get about your inner greatness.

So I decided, *I am delusional and insanely aspirational!* I'd tell myself, *You're so full of yourself. You feel like a star but that doesn't mean you are one!* I would try to put myself back in my place. *You have zero talents! You don't sing or dance well enough, you didn't even make the freshman swim team after years of swimming on teams. You're not an actress or a comedian; what do you even do? Who would give you a stage?*

This harsh dream-crushing dialogue did not come from anyone around me or my parents. They do not speak like this to themselves or anyone else! In fact they fearlessly modeled, and still do, going after your interests and dreams. And still, that harsh inner dialogue and my bold sense of self have been battling inside me for as long as I can remember.

I wrote this a few weeks ago in my phone:

> There's two Alisons. The one writing the book in flow
> and faith and love, believing everything is working
> together for the greatest good! And then the one
> sobbing in her car because the suffering, the pain, the
> confusion, the trying to let go, it's all just so difficult.
> The first one is always committing to things that make
> the second Alison want to die.

My husband teases me that I often talk about myself as two people. But maybe that's why the idea of consciousness and not being the voice inside my head makes so much sense to me. I want more of that first Alison! Awesome Alison!

Throughout my life there's been the flashes of peace, clarity, and expansion that are so freaking concrete to me! They come from a place of intuition, inner knowing, and feeling guided, and it makes sense to me that it would be my "true" state. What you might call your highest self.

That part, my awesome, my highest self, my witness, knew the exact man to marry, when to have babies, when the mood was just right for a giant dance party, or when to quit everything that was providing my current income and start a branding workshop and podcast instead. And that flowy faith-filled part did it with hardly a cognitive thought, refusing to ask silly little questions, like *How will you pay your bills?*

But the other part used to speak to me louder and more consistently. Unraveling the decisions I had made with clarity, making them start to feel impossible after the fact, the harsh voice would hiss this lie over and over and over: *You are not enough. You are not qualified, how dare you? WHO DO YOU THINK YOU ARE?!*

After speaking to so many people about their hopes, dreams, businesses, and lives, it's been a relief to see most of us have that part. Some people listen to it more than others. But we all have it. And it masquerades itself in your life in so many different ways. It's so sneaky, and it so easily makes you feel like what it's saying is truth.

So I've got a trick for you, on how to recognize it, and label it for what it is, which is FEAR. And the trick is this. Fear will always tell you this lie: "You don't get to show up as you are."

It might say it like this though:

- You need to find something more flattering to wear before you go to that party!

- You need to lose weight before you attend that conference!

- You have to have a bigger social media following before you reach out to that person!

- You need a partner, someone to hold hands with before you go there!

- You should get a nicer car, house, purse, shoes, or phone before you can . . .

Think of the way we talk about our bodies: You better tighten that, you better return that to "normal," you need to get your body back! You need thicker hair, longer lashes, more defined arms, straighter teeth . . . all before you can, you can what?

Breathe? Be allowed to exist? Be allowed to dream and feel valuable? You have to do all that before you can show up?! No wonder so many of us are too overwhelmed and exhausted to show up!

"Well, Alison," you start to protest, "I do need more experience before I can do this job I want because . . ."

Okay, for argument's sake, *maybe* you do. But also, odds are you're not looking to be a brain surgeon. Are you? If yes, please get whatever training is required. Other than that, I'm absolutely positive you're closer to your dream than you're able to even fathom. Take it from the girl who gave herself her own "show" and has had people agree that I'm a baking, crafting, events, branding, and "awesome" expert. You are one or two, or even ten or eleven, terrifying steps away from your dream.

And I have some incredibly good news! You don't have to be any different than you are, right now, to show up and take those steps. Which is why I say this over and over: Only you can be you, and you're already as awesome as you need to be!

The better news? You don't even need to figure out the steps you need to get to your dream! When you connect to your awesome, to your inner knowing, or your highest self, you will clearly see the actions arise in front of you. You won't have to push, force, hustle, coerce, or inflict suffering on yourself to show up as YOU and take those steps! You simply need to trust the truth of this shift: *I get to show up as I am, right now!* If you can believe it, you'll start to release the suffocating security blanket of fear that you've been wrapping around your own head.

DAMN, RIGHT?!

The work won't be forcing and shaming yourself to get out of bed, put down the sugar, and do the push-ups and to-dos. Nope. The tasks will flow with ease after you do the real work of transforming anxiety to flow, control to surrender, and quieting your hustle to a hush, so you can listen to the awesome voice of inner knowing and greatness that's inside of you!

There will still be lots of pain and discomfort as you expand and stretch. That's why we try not to label pain and discomfort as wrong or bad! Because this kind of pain and discomfort is growing you into who you dream of being. But you can't do any of it if you're too tired, unsure, beat up, or terrified to SHOW UP.

Which is why this shift is *I get to show up as I am,* right now! I had to add the "right now" because if I don't, we subconsciously add the caveats, right? So now we know there's no ifs, ands, or buts! Your beautiful butt gets to show up to your dreams, your relationships, your work, your conversations, your family, your life, exactly as it is, right this very minute.

Equating Suffering with Worth

Do you equate suffering with worth? Maybe Viktor Frankl's quote from *Man's Search for Meaning* resonates with you: "To suffer unnecessarily is masochistic rather than heroic."

Even though I have been lucky enough to make a career, like I dreamed I might, of speaking and teaching on stages, it has (which I'm sure will not shock you at all at this point) caused me insane amounts of suffering and anxiety.

One of the many reasons is that somewhere along the line I picked up the belief that the more I suffer, the better I will be.

And the more I suffer when I create something, the better, that is, more worthy and defendable, the thing will be too. Meaning, the more suffering I can make it through, the more glory! The better the product or result! The more proof it's okay I got the thing! It's a self-masochistic way of "earning" the good things in your life. You know, to make sure you're worthy of them. (Remember, you're worthy of them no matter what!)

Let's just check in real quick to see if you picked up this lie too. Take a moment to inhale, and then exhale. How does that feel in your body? The idea that you need to suffer, change, be better, or different before you get to show up? And the more you suffer, the better and more worthy you'll be?

Yikes! It runs so deeply in me my arms tighten with anxious tension and I have to pause to slow and observe my breath. What does it do for you? It's okay if it does nothing! Just something to watch!

And what's also fun is watching how many different ways that same lie—that you have to suffer or be different or better to show up, that it's not okay to be yourself—will disguise itself to show up in your life!

We often label it with the word *comparison*.

DID YOU SEE THAT ONE COMING?!

Honestly I don't know if you did, but I'm excited about it. And I'm also so excited about this Danish proverb: "If envy were a fever, all the world would be ill."

Escape the Comparison Trap

I laugh so hard when my four-year-old, (the terrifying and terrific) Fiona, wants me to listen to her. She grabs my face with both her hands, physically turns my head to be square with hers, and isn't satisfied until I'm staring deep into her eyes repeating back every word she says in confirmation. I relate to this on every level. I've been speaking and demanding people give me their undivided attention for over thirty years; like I said, I love to chat! And I've been speaking professionally and demanding payment for it (politely, I'm sure) for over six years.

I'm going to level with you, I'm really good at it. I'm worth what I charge and I bring something unique to the stage beyond the fact I will always air hump and occasionally crawl across it. In fact, much of this book has been created from the concepts I share and teach when I speak. I've definitely put in my ten thousand hours through classes, practice, teaching, creating videos and podcasts, and doing free gigs for a long time.

A few years back I was hired to speak at a corporate conference in Southern California, and I was excited because it aligned perfectly with another business conference that I wanted to attend. Why? Because Queen Goddess Brené Brown was the headline speaker. Sold! I booked the speaking gig for myself and packed jumpsuits for both conferences.

To say I love Brené Brown would be putting it mildly. And while loving her has become a cliché written into Netflix movies, the love she attracts runs so deep because of how bravely and boldly she shows up as herself and shares her truth.

The way the weekend's schedule lined up, I would have *just* enough time to hit up Goddess Brené's keynote, then take a car across L.A. to deliver a keynote of my own to an audience of about five hundred people.

I got to the ballroom early, with as much excitement as I had at my very first *NSYNC concert. And as Brené spoke, my jaw hit the floor. How could my love for this woman deepen even more?! Oh, but it did! She commanded the room in her clogs and Southwest jewelry with the expertise of a precision sniper, her years and years of college teaching experience pouring through her. I laughed, I cried, I was uplifted, I learned, I was changed for the better, I felt all the feelings a human wants to in a sixty-minute period. The room was electric with energy and united in the experience. It was truly a gift to witness.

And then I remembered that I had to go grab a car, get my butt across town, and speak on my own stage next. Thankfully not to the same room, but after witnessing what could be, I felt like what I had to offer was a giant pile of crap.

How did I even con people into paying me to speak when Brené Brown exists on this planet?! My usual prespeaking nerves began to climb to a fever pitch.

I know the danger of comparison gets talked about often. Comparison is the thief of joy, yada, yada, yada. Don't compare yourself to other people on social media. Don't compare yourself to your neighbor or the Kardashians, and, duh, don't compare yourself to Brené Brown.

And before you check out and say, "Heard it!" or "I've already worked on comparison, and I don't do it!" (insert your hair flip here!), listen up, because I find the sneakiest type of comparison, the kind we don't think to watch out for, but the one that takes out incredibly glorious individuals like you and me, is comparing your current self to the version of yourself you think you SHOULD be, or should be by now.

It's the part of you that says, *You don't get to show up as you! You need to do X before you do!*

Of course I felt inadequate as a speaker compared to Brené

Brown. But what I was really upset about was that I was not at her level . . . yet. Deep down, as Brené and that vision I had of myself all those years ago taught me, I dare greatly, I dare to lead. I believe that I have the capacity to speak on her level.

But what could I not stop beating myself up about? Why did I feel like I did not get to show up, in that moment?

Because I was not there YET. I wasn't that future version of myself right now. How dare I not already be at that level, what had I been wasting my time doing? And how could I justify getting up on a stage as the half-baked, gooey-in-the-center cake that I am?

We are a species that relies on social interactions to survive. Therefore comparison is inevitable. It has helped us stay alive, and the primitive brain wants to put everything in boxes. Specifically the "similar" and "different" boxes, which invites comparison all day every day.

But as you work to evolve past those black-and-white perimeters and live out of your inherent awesomeness, the comparison trap evolves too.

We begin to compare ourselves to past and future versions of ourselves. Even parallel versions of ourselves, the person we like to fantasize we would have been if we had made different choices, weighed less, or if different things had happened to us or circumstances and the world were different.

It is a trap because it keeps us prisoner in the past or in the future. But the present moment is the only place from which we can take action. The present moment is the only place where you can shift your thoughts, decide to stop beating yourself up, forgive yourself, and choose love.

The present moment is the only place we can escape the

comparison trap and hear our inner knowing whisper what step to take next.

On the ride over to my keynote I was gifted one of the finest ride-share drivers I've ever met, Richard. We launched into a deep conversation, my favorite thing to do with my ride-share drivers, about dreams, talents, goals, and hopes. Richard was curious about my job, where I was going, and why I was insistent on encouraging him to start a ride-share conversation-based podcast. He had such a gift for gab! And was so wise!

I told Richard I was going to speak at a conference, hence all the glitter on my eyes, and that I was pretty nervous and feeling inadequate.

Richard then shared the most beautiful story with me that has continued to bless my life and the lives of thousands of people I've been able to share it with.

Richard was in his fifties and had been married a couple times. During his first marriage he said he was married to a woman from a very religious family, and they had a very hard time accepting that she had married a man with a different background and faith. He said family gatherings were filled with tension and awkwardness. Richard told me that rather than going into family get-togethers and deciding that everyone disliked him and didn't want him in the family, he would say to himself, *Everyone loves you and is so glad you're here.*

He told me to get up on that stage and say to myself, *Everyone loves me and they are so glad I'm here!*

We cried together. We hugged, and he dropped me off. And I was armed with what has now become one of my best mantras for social anxiety, nervousness, and allowing myself to believe I get to show up as I am, right now!

Everyone Loves Me and Is So Glad I'm Here

I believe the magic in these words is they bring us into acceptance with our present self. *Everyone loves me, and they are so glad I'm here.* This thought is the skeleton key to the comparison trap.

To take it one step further, "I love myself, and I'm so glad I'm here" is the underlying sentiment that gives this statement its power. When we love ourselves, we accept ourselves. And when we more fully accept ourselves, comparison loses its luster. I accept myself in the moment. I accept you in the moment. I accept the moment.

Anxiety begins to dissipate, and there is the letting go that is required to STOP BEATING YOURSELF UP, and let yourself just be who you currently are.

Now when I am nervous about a speaking job, feeling stupid at a dinner party, or getting self-conscious in my own skin, I say to myself, *Everyone loves me, they're so glad I'm here!* The beauty of it is it makes no difference whether it's true or not. Remember: how other people feel about you is something you cannot control anyway. It invites you to show up comfortably, without defense, without the need to judge or dominate, to puff up and prove.

Try it! Try saying this and NOT getting more love for everyone you meet. I've found it impossible. As I say it to myself over and over, I start to notice that my next inclination is to extend that enthusiasm and love to anyone I encounter.

To the man passing me at the airport I think, *Everyone loves you and is so glad YOU are here!*

To the woman helping me check in for my flight I try to telepathically beam, *Everyone loves YOU and is so glad you're here!*

Then what starts to happen? I notice that I start treating anyone I'm having a small interaction with, with more love. In other words, I begin to become more of the type of person everyone really could love and would be so excited to have around.

In Richard's case, he said he knew it wasn't true when he started thinking it, he knew his extended family didn't initially have warm feelings for him. They were not glad he was there. But he said that after a while, continuing to show up with this belief, he was able to establish genuine relationships with most of the people in his wife's family. He joked that they started to like him more than his wife!

Armed with a hug from Richard and his advice, I got up onstage, feeling much better, and I shared his words with the audience. Now at most keynotes I have everyone turn to each other, look the other person in the eye, and say, "I'm so glad you're here."

This also helped me get filled back up with love and gratitude for Brené Brown. And rather than being stuck in a trap of comparison with her, or her skill set versus my current skill set, I was able to appreciate that I had just witnessed a great woman stand in her power. And I was able to bring the fire and light she had shared with me onstage to five hundred more women. I feel like that's what Brené would want! I know that's what I would want. And what a bummer it would have been if I would have missed feeling that in favor of feeling like crap stuck in comparison.

Tools You Can Use Now!

Believing the shift *I get to show up as I am, right now!* is easy to practice every day.

When you're having a conversation, and share a true opinion that feels vulnerable, you can say, *It's okay to be myself, even if they don't agree. Just like it's okay for them to be who they are, even if I don't agree.*

Why is it okay? Because your value is not determined by people agreeing with you. You are the witness, you are not the thoughts.

The questions and ideas we just talked about can help prevent the spiral of fear too. To recap:

- ◑ Do I believe I have to suffer to be worthy?

- ◑ What limits or qualifications am I putting on myself before I get to show up?

- ◑ Am I comparing who I am right now to who I think I should be?

- ◑ And the mantra that Richard shares: "Everybody loves me and is so glad I'm here!" You can ask yourself, even if you don't believe it, how would me believing this serve me or the world around me?

Now when I start to spiral before a speaking gig, I TAP. Sometimes I tune in and accept that fear is popping up because I'm about to do something vulnerable that will expand me. Usually I tune in and accept that control has hijacked my sanity and wants me to believe if I worry or stress enough I can control how everyone perceives me and how they'll feel. When I accept these feelings rather than trying to beat them or force them out of myself, they can pass through me. So I can pick my focus, which when I speak is always "light." *Let my heart speak light to their hearts* is my prayer. *May I get out of the way from what I think people need and saying things that I think will make me look good, so I can be open to what each room really needs to allow those who are ready or I am meant to touch, to feel light.*

It doesn't mean that every single speaking gig is full of only people who love me, and I've magically figured out a way to only get positive results, which for me means every single person is obsessed with me and tells me as much with lavish praise. I thought it might. But it doesn't.

What my prayer, my intention, does is instead give me a goal that invites me to feel my awesomeness. Getting my ego out of the way, believing I can be guided, and striving to bask in light and love so I can more clearly reflect others light and love has created a process that refines and changes me. And even though I want to fight this often, at the end of the day that's what I've decided is my personal success. Because it's one of the only things I can control, how I approach the process, not the results.

Acceptance Is an Incredible Gift

Acceptance is an incredible gift. One we often give so stingily! To ourselves and to others. Why? Many reasons I think, but mostly the lie. The lie that none of us are okay as we are. The lie that to be more, do more, have more, be accepted, have love, have success, have safety, we need to change. We think it's true for ourselves, and therefore true for all.

Believing that you are okay to be yourself, that you get to show up as you are, brings you back to your awesome; it doesn't just combat the lie, it makes it irrelevant.

The more delighted and okay I am with myself, the more delighted I am when other people are themselves. Even when that "self" rubs up against me in an abrasive way, even when them being themselves is the polar opposite of what I believe to be "good." And so if we want to give the gift of what it feels like to just be accepted and to be okay, showing up grumpy, showing up snappy, showing up depressed, showing up anxious, showing up with joy, showing up with bubbliness—we accept ourselves.

When we sit in a place of awareness, when we sit in our awesome, not the mind and the constructs of ego and self we have created, we are more open. We're able to see ourselves more clearly because we're not so afraid of what we're going to see. And when we're not so afraid of what we're going to see, we can really look at ourselves.

And we can be gentle with ourselves, and who we are right now.

And this gentleness, this understanding, this acceptance is desperately needed because it is not safe for some people to be themselves. Due to the color of their skin, who they love, where they live. Maybe it wasn't physically safe for you to be yourself in your family, with your loved ones, or in your country. Maybe this feels impossible because in so many ways it is. It is because we've been limited by the world of form, by believing that we and other people are our thoughts, our minds, our ideas. We believe it so firmly that we kill for our sense of identity, we suppress and dominate to assert our physical, limited sense of greatness.

Because we don't feel our true awesomeness, our awareness, our expansiveness, our hugeness!

Here's how I see it: the more of us who have relative safety, or can get ourselves to safety, the more of us who stand up and claim, "It's okay to be myself. I get to show up as I am, RIGHT NOW!," the faster we can make it a better world. The more you believe it is safe and okay to be you, the more you will be inspired to make it safe for other people to be themselves, to help them feel their inherent power, to release judgment and not be divided. When you realize you do not need to dominate or control anyone to feel awesome or to have true peace, you, as Gandhi said, "be the change you wish to see in the world."

You get to show up, as you are, right now! You get to use your voice, no matter how low and scratchy it is, to live the life of your dreams. It will be uncomfortable, it will expose and stretch you, but it will also invite more joy, more growth, and more beauty into your life, and consequently the world. Come on now, what's better than that?

11

I'm Being Guided and Supported!

There's some good in this world . . .
and it's worth fighting for.

—SAMWISE GAMGEE IN *LORD OF THE RINGS*

My sister, Andrea, and I are only sixteen months apart, and we were always treated like twins growing up. I was mistakenly called "Andrea" or "An—Alison" so much at church or school, that if I'm in a crowd and someone says the name "Andrea" I'll still, to this day, turn around and look to see who's asking for me.

Andrea runs a successful natural soap company called Tubby Todd with her husband, Brian, and because we're both entrepreneurs and share our personalities online, people often think, just like they did when we were growing up, that we're exactly the same. I always say, "Socially and when you first meet us we are very similar! But at our core we are almost polar opposites."

It's hard to see your siblings in their true light. Especially younger siblings, it can be difficult to allow them to be more than what they are in your family order and dynamics.

But I'll never forget seeing one of Andrea's superpowers clearly emerge early on in her business when she was hosting an event to celebrate her company, Tubby Todd, launching in a retail space. She lives in Southern California and I had flown from my home in Utah to help her run and set up the event, which of course included a mini dance party in the retail shop.

For the event's photo op, Andrea had found a vintage clawfoot tub. We were going to fill it with clear balloons and set a bubble machine by it, inviting partygoers to have some good, clean fun! Small and often distracted, Andrea is a slightly terrifying driver. So I nervously held on as she transferred me and the roughly five-hundred-plus-pound tub in a borrowed pickup truck to the venue. As we got closer I said, "So what's the plan?"

"The plan for what?" Andrea asked.

"For getting the bathtub out of the truck and into the venue. Do they have people there who can lift it? Did you hire some moving guys to meet us?" I was so confused. There was no way we could move this beast of a bathtub.

"Oh, I just thought we'd figure it out when we get there!" she said optimistically.

I started getting really upset. "What? That thing is huge! We need multiple people! How did you get it in the truck?"

She started laughing, "Oh, Mitt Romney and some other people put it in there!"

"Mitt Romney, who ran for president?"

"Yeah! When I went to pick up the bathtub, he was at the house so I just asked all the people there if they would help lift it! See, it will be fine."

"Andrea! This is going to take forever! Why wouldn't you hire someone?! It's so heavy no one is going to just lift it! This is going to set us back so much time . . ."

She ignored me, in true little sister style, and as we pulled up to the venue she said, "It's fine. I'll do it."

Within minutes she had the small retail space prepped with the double doors open wide. She opened the back of the truck and just kind of waited. A road biker in spandex shorts and full gear was zooming by and Andrea said, "Sir! Oh my gosh! We are trying to move this tub, and it looks like you're obviously in good shape, can you help?"

I was legitimately hiding in the truck cab, refusing to get out. I was cringing as Andrea asked this random man for help. The biker was kind of confused, but he just said, "Okay."

It was early in the morning and the store's neighboring restaurants and shops weren't fully open. So there weren't many people around. But this didn't stop Andrea. She knocked on the door of an unopened restaurant and said she needed help moving a giant tub. It was a Mexican restaurant and most of the people there at that time didn't speak English. Luckily Andrea, fluent in Spanish, waltzed to the back of the kitchen and politely asked the kitchen crew if they could please help.

Yes, I was still in the car, hiding. Jaw on the floor. Mortified by, but also now superimpressed with, Andrea. Within moments the kitchen crew and the biker were all happily, yes, happily, helping move an incredibly heavy bathtub. They were genuinely delighted to be of service. Andrea thanked everyone and I finally got out of the car.

The party was a success, the photo op was perfect, and the whole celebration ended with a conga line through the street as we waved to the restaurant workers and they danced to the music we were blasting.

Now I get it, Andrea was a young, cute blonde. You might be thinking, *Even if I did this, no one would help me.* Maybe, maybe not. I've learned people will surprise you, in both good ways and bad. But we both objectively had the exact same resources in this scenario. One of us got the tub moved, and one of us hid embarrassed in the car.

The one hiding in the car is the same person who has zero shame crawling across a stage or thrusting for thousands on the internet. The same person who wore whatever she wanted in high school and refuses to feel bad if her kids get absolutely none of their schoolwork done, as long as they are kind and respectful. I feel zero embarrassment when my mother-in-law asks, "Did you mean to brush the back of your hair?" And when I constantly get praised for being "So brave!" for not wearing makeup or having a clean house on lots of my social media posts.

I'm not brave for showing up looking exactly as I look. That requires little vulnerability from me. But going to a doctor? Getting a diagnosis? Asking for help from someone I'm not paying or don't feel like I can benefit in some way? Hell to the no.

Most of my breaking points around my accident came from accepting help. I remember when my eighty-year-old next-door neighbor brought us dinner, I started sobbing. She could barely walk herself, and yet she showed up with a pizza. I had apologized and apologized to the paramedics, thanking them as much as I apologized in my blurry, dizzy state.

My lead paramedic was a man named Regan. He was both clearly amused and confused by me trying to deny I needed to get in an ambulance, and he was the one who caught me as I slumped over to pass out. While I kept apologizing as he transferred me out of the ambulance to the ER, he finally said, "Letting people help you is a talent."

Dammit, Regan! Hitting me with truth that hard, minutes after being hit by a car?! Savage.

But it stuck.

Letting people help you is one of the greatest talents any human can have. It's also a skill I've noticed all the most successful people I know have. They build their families with more ease, build businesses faster, and live with more fun.

The shift *I'm being guided and supported* not only shifts your perspective from one of lack to one of abundance, from one of loneliness to connection, it also invites you to feel awesome by recognizing you don't have to do any of this life alone.

Do we not ask for help because it feels vulnerable? Do we not ask for help because we believe we don't deserve it? Do we not ask for help because we think we are so special and unique in our problems that no one can solve them?

Why don't you ask for help? Maybe someone told you you couldn't when you were a child? Maybe you were ignored when you've asked for help in the past or you couldn't see anyone to ask?

Maybe we're just tired. We tried. We made the doctor appointment, we tried the medication. We didn't like the way they made us feel, it didn't help.

Or maybe like me, people just didn't listen. Couldn't hear what you were saying between the jokes and downplaying. Maybe they heard but I couldn't see it? I didn't give them enough of a chance?

For most of my life I suspected my period wasn't like lots of other women's. But I also just dismissed myself as being dramatic. I had my hormones tested, and took some hormone supplements for a while, but it only kind of helped and I just hate doctors' appointments. Every few years I'd try again. I'd explain my symptoms and they'd say, "Oh, we can just make your period go away with this pill."

So I took the pill, and then monthly I'd get all the symptoms still. Suicidal thoughts, impossible cramps, nights of no sleep, not being able to stop thinking everyone hates me and everything I say is the worst. But then I wouldn't get the period that helped release all that. It was horrible. I stopped listening to the doctors; they couldn't help me.

After giving birth, fueled with so much adrenaline and anxiety, I wouldn't sleep at all. Postpartum anxiety and depression debilitated me from feeling much other than panic. After my first baby, I took their damn pills. Trying to figure out if they were helping or hurting sent me into the lowest places I've ever been.

The closest I ever got to really hurting myself was when I was pregnant with my second baby, going on and off antianxiety medication without a therapist or supervision. The group of midwives I attended did not understand how serious I was when I said I wanted to die. It was a dark time.

With my third baby I was determined not to suffer so much, I wasn't going to let it get so bad. I wanted different results so I changed it all up. I got a therapist before I got pregnant. I got a family practitioner so the same person would see me, and I had my husband go with me to every appointment so when I downplayed symptoms he could jump in. Overall, the pregnancy was better. But afterward, it was more of the same.

I called my doctor; he said it was just baby blues, that they'd go away, and if they didn't in a week, to call back. I couldn't imagine being alive for another week, but I didn't say that, I just got off the phone in tears. I couldn't push more than that. I emailed my therapist; she dismissed me. I had done what I could do.

Fiona was born in December. I threw my next dance party in March, nursing her in between hanging hundreds of cardboard gems for "Alison's Gem Jam": for ladies who rock.

I don't know, guys, after writing a book, and hosting a podcast with millions and millions of downloads, I feel safe to say: I'm a pretty good communicator. But I've explained the same symptoms, both frantically and calmly, to lots of different specialists. The language of receiving help, and allowing others to help me, is one of the hardest things I've had to learn. If for you, like my sister, it comes more easily, consider yourself blessed. Like Regan the paramedic said, "Letting people help you is a talent." Like any other talent, I think some of us are born with a more natural ability. But regardless of that, it's something we can all develop.

Seeing and allowing ourselves to be guided and supported is not just something we can develop, it's something we *must* develop if we want to show up as our truest, most expansive selves.

We cannot give beyond what we are willing to receive. As the wonderful Wayne Dyer said, "You can't give what you don't have."

If you want to give help without judgment, you need to be able to receive help without judgment. If you want to support other people in their journeys of healing, you need to allow yourself, without shame, to be guided and lifted in your own journey of healing.

In my Build an Awesome Brand workshop, when asked the

"why" of their businesses, I'd say at least 70 percent of the students say they want to inspire people.

To that I say, "No one wants to be inspired AT. They want to be inspired BY." The "at" is the telling, the preaching, the inspirational quotes that you understand but do not practice. The inspired "by" requires vulnerability. It requires us to do the hard work of healing, overcoming, breaking, and rebuilding, and doing it all absolutely imperfectly.

Receiving Versus Getting

When I was growing up, you could see how loved or popular someone was by how much birthday loot they carried around at school. I guess the equivalent now is social media followers? But in the late 1990s and early 2000s, it was balloons, bouquets of flowers, oversize cards, and gift bags carried around on your day of birth with pride. Lugging it all from class to class, making a tiny scene getting it all settled in each new period.

If someone shared your birthday date, you could directly compare. And you could also get pretty petty about it: *Oh, her balloon bouquet is so big but it's all from, like, one person, so that's why it seems like so much.*

On my birthday last year I said to my husband, "I'm just stressed because I don't know what to do, like I'm really busy with the book and don't need to do a whole thing. I don't want to see a lot of people but a couple are asking what my plans are. Do I invite the people who don't seem to care?"

He started laughing and said, "What are you making your birthday mean?"

I started laughing, too, because I knew. "I'm making it mean that the more balloons and flowers I get to carry around in the halls, the better person I must be. The more people must love me and that means I'm a good friend and therefore 'good.'"

But I'm not good because flowers and balloons declare it so. You are not worthy of love or help because people offer it or do not offer it.

My whole life I think I believed I could only get help if my suffering proved it was bad enough. And because enough is a decision, not an amount, I had decided my suffering was never enough.

You are not being guided and supported because you've earned it. You're being guided and supported because you are inherently and wholly awesome. It's always there, even if you can't physically see it or carry it. Even if doctors keep dismissing you or not being able to help. You keep showing up for yourself, and work on being ready to receive.

I'm not a sixteen-year-old girl anymore who needs flowers and cards to know she's enough. So for my birthday I decided to let go. To receive and allow any love that wanted to find its way to me, to find me.

In this way, I've noticed there is a difference between getting and receiving.

If you make getting mean something about your value, you'll always be noting, counting, weighing out your worth in the actions of others. This way of calculating worth is directly tied to not allowing yourself to have help or kindness without self-judgment.

Receiving, on the other hand, is about allowing, surrendering, and being part of the exchange.

When I realized how much my Instagram comments and numbers were dictating my mood and sense of worth, I thought, *I need to make them mean nothing about me!* So

I detached. Or so I thought. What I really did was numb it out. I refused to receive it. Yes, I stopped taking the hurtful comments or decline in numbers quite so personally, but I also numbed out and blocked a lot of good. *They can't mean anything about me!* I thought, so I didn't allow them into my heart.

I was being a crappy receiver. You can receive and allow love, help, guidance, and support without attaching your value to it. What happens instead is you see it for what it is, the flow of energy and love that is swirling around you!

When you receive, you do so with gratitude. Without expectation. Without noticing who you got the love from and who forgot to call.

I walked around my whole birthday, receiving text messages, phone calls, and gifts. And with each one I was just floored. "I am so greatly loved!" I kept shouting. "Everybody loves me!"

My older brother called me two weeks later, horrified he'd forgotten my birthday. I didn't even notice.

Prevent the Spiral

Listen to the Still, Small Voice of Your Inner Knowing

During one of the lockdown phases of the pandemic, I was driving home, on the same road where I was hit. Not far past the site of my accident I again saw all the bad lights.

Fire trucks, police cars, and an ambulance. I didn't want to be a lookie-loo, but I know most of the people in those houses so I became intensely worried. A little while later we found out a young dad, who had been living with his parents while he was going through a divorce, had taken his own life. We knew him, some of his siblings, his two young daughters, and his parents.

It has never been difficult for me to understand why someone would take their own life. For so much of my life whenever a suicide was reported in the news my heart would break but simultaneously I'd think, *I get that, I get it.*

The instant I heard of my neighbor's tragic death I dropped to my knees and asked, *What can I do, who can I serve?* I was guided and supported as these words flowed to me as I posted them on Instagram, hoping that they'd reach one person who might need to hear them:

"I want to say this to anyone who will hear: You touch more hearts than you could ever know. You are a positive influence, a light, a smile, an anchor to more hearts than you can possibly imagine.

"If you can't feel it, it's okay. Just know we need you. AS YOU. Hang in there, don't quit. Don't quit on yourself. Don't quit on this earth even when it feels like it has quit on you.

"Hold on. Hold on. You affect more people—for good, for beauty, for the better—than you know. You are an important part of this bigger whole. Will you think about someone who might not be able to feel this truth right now and text them a little word of love? And if you HEAR me, love to you, too."

Later I thought, but what about his family? I didn't have any inspiration on what I could do there. *When you'll need it, you'll have it*, I felt my highest self say. Weeks later I saw his mom in passing and I was flooded with direction for a small gesture: *Take them one of the peach cobblers you just made. With a basket of self-care products for her. You've got all those lotions and bath salts.*

I used to feel like an idiot doing these things. Questioning myself the whole time. But not so much anymore. I made the gift basket, and some bold fringe earrings I had in my gifts-to-give drawer, which I constantly stock with things I find for exact occasions like this, caught my eye. His mom is in her sixties and I felt a little sheepish choosing earrings for her, but I thought, *Why argue at this point? You're this far in.* We dropped off the cobbler and the gift basket.

It doesn't take much to think of and put into action a small gesture of kindness for someone; in fact, I'm sure you've done something like this too. The point is when you feel that direction, that tug, that impulse to do or say something, trust it and do what it says.

NOW! The most important part of this shift is I'm being guided and supported to act with intention and without expectation. Act without confirmation from some outside source. This can look like reaching out to a person you felt guided to reach out to. You listened to your inner knowing! Did it come from a place of expansion? Did it come from a place of love and calm? Then you're good. That's all you need. Occasionally the Universe throws you a bone too. In this case that happened. His mom wrote me a thank-you card saying how much she loved the earrings specifically and how they reminded her it was okay to feel some joy, even in that dark time.

You Are Being Guided and Supported

I've started a new path for healing and hope with my hormones. I've allowed myself to be guided and directed. I tell myself when I go to the appointments, *This might not give you all the results and solutions you want, but that doesn't mean it wasn't inspired.*

I write down how I feel in low times, and I track my cycles and note my symptoms from my place as the witness. From my AWESOME. I try not to attach to the feelings and darkness that start to swallow me monthly as I work with different health practitioners to not dip so low.

Here are a few things I've learned:

- You'll often need to ask for help more than once, from more than one person, and that's okay.

- The sooner you allow help and guidance, the sooner you'll find relief. You're worthy of healing.

- If you don't feel like a therapist, doctor, or medication is helping you, speak up. You can do so with kindness, and find a new practitioner.

- Your healing and help are a path, not a destination. Each thing you try and allow is a step; don't give up if that step isn't the cure-all.

- There's no magic marker of sickness; why not rule things out instead of waiting and proving?

- Receiving, allowing, and surrendering to help is a gift you give the world.

Ultimately, I've learned that what helps is admitting you can't often see yourself clearly, and outside help is a necessary step in easing suffering. If you feel like you can't afford it, or don't have access, speak up when you feel brave enough and directed to do so. Identify the need, voice it, and believe the shift *I'm being guided and supported*. Take notes and write down whenever you see it happening. You will be guided to a path or person that can help.

You'll hear the guidance when you quiet your yapping mind, when you surrender and receive that love and light that are trying to find you.

Now when I have the infrequent panic attack, I feel guided and connected even while hyperventilating. I'll hear, *Text Julie* (my friend) or *Ask Eric to hold you*. I'll sob and say while I allow the panic to move through me, *You're doing so good. You're doing so good having this anxiety attack. You're strong for having this, not weak.*

Or when my raging PMDD period hormones want me to quit writing, I instead make notes in my phone like this: "Your book might be garbage. But you are not garbage. Your butt might look like garbage, but you are not garbage. You feel like garbage. But you are not garbage. You are not garbage."

In your doubt, you're still being guided and supported by your inner knowing, your awesome, your highest self. In your fear, in your loneliness, in your anxiety and depression, that expansive, light-soaked part of you is still always there preparing a way for you. Your job is to feel that awesome now, and to receive it. You can do it; I know you can. I'm cheering for you as you do.

12

Joy Has Big Plans for Me!

If you carry joy in your heart,
you can heal any moment.

—CARLOS SANTANA

My husband, Eric, is the most wonderful gardener. He tends to his garden boxes of vegetables, herbs, and melons, his houseplants, and the various trees and flower beds all over our yard with the patience and understanding of a monk. Whether he decides to build a minipond, fill it with turtles and koi, and plant ground covering for future lushness, or build a trellis for hanging plants and crawling vines, he has some sort of impossible innate confidence that things will grow and work out. And they always do!

Our house is filled with his green goodness, pathos dripping down many walls, and rubber plants proudly fanning out their dark broad glossy leaves. I used to roll my eyes when another plant snuck its way onto a bookshelf, or I'd come home from work to find boxes of even more trees freshly delivered from some funny discount site. I'd tease him, and like Eric usually does, he'd laugh good-naturedly, take nothing personally, and keep doing exactly what he wants to do.

After years of mostly ambivalence, I've noticed that as my inner world centers more on flow rather than anxiety, and craves quiet over stimulation, that the plants call to me and calm me. And I've become very invested in all the life that's growing around me.

I walk up to our huge fiddle-leaf fig and examine each leaf, worriedly asking, "Is this how they're supposed to look? Is it dying? I see some brown?! This one is curling? Is it okay!?"

Eric barely glances at it and says, "It's fine. Leaves do that."

"But is it SUPPOSED to do that?!" I'll say, prodding and picking.

"It goes through cycles. It's healthy, it's a beautiful healthy tree." He says this completely unconcerned, continuing to do whatever I've interrupted him doing.

Eric is so sure of his connection with the plants. He doesn't spend hours online researching the exact way to care for each one, he just waters them. He doesn't get obsessed with soil needs and pH balances, he just pays attention and appreciates their beauty. He befriends elderly gardeners and gets advice from them. At home he nonchalantly praises the plants as he passes them and haphazardly pulls away old leaves. He's not precise, or overly careful, but he's consistent, deliberate, and thoughtful. Desperate, hopeful plant parents see our overgrowth and long to know how he's so successful. He never offers any ground-breaking advice.

I've started my own collection of plants in my office space, which of course means I beg Eric to come to my office and check on my plants and tell me if they're okay.

He swings by, and again I agonize over each leaf that's anything other than exactly pristine, saying, "BUT WHAT ABOUT THIS ONE?!"

"Yeah, sweetie, leaves die," he'll say as he laughs. "Just give it time, try more or less water next time, let's see what happens."

It's hard for me to be patient with the plants, as I've never been patient about basically anything. Patience is a trait I've had to cultivate from scratch, it feels like there's not naturally an ounce of it in my body. But patience, I've learned, is just another way of describing acceptance, allowance, and surrender. To be patient, you need to be present and allow each leaf of your life to be what it is.

I believe that Eric is such a fantastic gardener because of his beautiful patience. But just as important, if not even more so, is his hope and vision of the beauty each plant holds, and his faith that it will come to fruition.

He is the perfect example of cultivating and allowing joy. Like any true master gardener, he has big plans for what he sows. He hopes for each seed's fullest expansion and expression into beauty and greatness.

The shift *Joy has big plans for me!* fills my heart with hope and requires patience. It asks me to have vision beyond my narrow understanding, and it inspires faith. Faith in the gardener of joy, faith that joy has big plans for me, and faith that following joy will lead me to my fullest expansion and expression of my deepest, truest, highest self.

We Are Not Defined by
Our Pain or Mistakes

Sometimes it hurts to believe that joy is available to you. It doesn't just feel like joy is impossible, it doesn't just feel like joy will never come, the actual act of keeping the faith is physically painful. In this place, no matter how many times I sing along with Wilson Phillips, it's hard to believe I can "Hold on for one more day." It feels like an invitation to torture.

When you're in that much pain, it can be incredibly hard to believe that you're not doing something wrong. That life just shouldn't feel this way. That you shouldn't feel this way, that something must be terribly off.

The other night my sweet Rad came up after he was supposed to be asleep. He starts to melt into the ground when he's tired, and he also gets very sad. He told me he didn't know what he was feeling or why he was sad. I asked my sneaky mom questions to make sure everything at school and in his life is safe. All seemed well, so I said, "That's okay, buddy, you don't have to know why. It's okay to be sad." And then he looked up at me with the biggest tears pouring down his perfectly poreless face, and said, "I think something is wrong, I think something is wrong with me because I feel this way."

I, of course, started crying with him. Because it's so hard to see someone you love be in such a specific type of pain you know so well.

I grabbed his tiny body clad in his dad's giant T-shirt. I squeezed him longer and harder than any eight-year-old wants to be held by their mom, and just said over and over, "You're not wrong to feel anything you feel. But I'm so sorry you have to feel such sad feelings. You're doing such a good job feeling them." If I could put up a billboard, that might be it.

You're not doing it wrong—parenting, your job, living your purpose. Like me, I'm sure you've made mistakes. But we don't need to add to life's suffering with shame and self-loathing. I promise you'll still grow and evolve and not be a monster if you love yourself.

I found this Léon Bloy quote in college and it has guided me for years: "There are places in the heart that do not yet exist, suffering has to enter in so they may come to be."

Your heart, in this exact moment, is so beautiful, so deep, and full of so many amazing complexities because of your unique life experience. The suffering that has broken it to pieces, and the love you've allowed into those cracks to make it whole—it's so incredibly glorious. I know deep within me, that if we allow it to, life creates the most beautiful labyrinths in our hearts. And those hearts are our greatest gift to the world, and ourselves.

Jump in the River of Joy

As I've talked about living in the flow, over and over, I've thought a lot about how to describe what that looks and feels like. Deciding to feel awesome now is like deciding to return to the river of joy, over and over and over.

Waking up to your awesome is remembering you are aware-ness, you can sit in the seat of the soul, you are light, you are expansive, and great. Every time you do this, every time you return to love and jump in that river of joy, it's a baptism. And you can be carried in the flow of love.

And like baptism by immersion symbolizes, when you dive

into the river of joy you die a sort of death. You let the old experiences, the old thoughts and judgments about yourself and this world die. And you're reborn in the presence of love.

Most of my life, I've placed my value in the hands of others and in my outside accomplishments. But every time I return to the river of joy, every time I decide to feel my awesomeness and surrender to the flow, I let that old self die, and more of who I really am is exposed.

Don't Let "Failure" Wreck You

In 2020, I had to downsize all but one full-time employee and most of my contract workers and let go of all my planned events and speaking gigs. So I felt beyond blessed to get one large corporate consulting contract. This was my only steady income, as all other revenue sources for my business had stopped dead in their tracks. The contract was for six months and was the only reason we could pay our bills.

I was so grateful for this large contract, and it felt like God was carrying me through this impossibly confusing dark time.

I also had one final mastermind event for my own clients, which was supposed to be an in-person weekend that we moved to a weekend of online group coaching instead. I was very, very stressed that I wouldn't be able to provide enough value through this online format. My tiny team and I were doing everything in our power to provide a magical digital experience for my coaching clients.

We'll call my corporate client Flower Pop. Flower Pop had a huge sales field, and I had done three very successful livestream trainings for them filled with rave reviews and record-breaking engagement for the company. The sales field was insanely enthusiastic, motivated, and warm. After each livestream, I received gobs of praise and calls from the CEO saying how pleased she was. The fourth month of the contract included me working with their very top leaders.

On Wednesday I hopped on a coaching call with about ten of Flower Pop's top salespeople. Immediately it felt off. It was nothing like the large livestreams, the salespeople were mostly standoffish, and there was a corporate executive on the call, who, despite my repeated attempts to engage and get feedback from, remained dead silent.

The call ended and though there had been one or two people who engaged, the rest were silent, almost afraid to answer questions, refusing to say that anything needed fixing or examining. One woman had been basically hostile with me. I chose to believe that was just her vibe.

On Thursday I had my own personal coaching mastermind session that I was very nervous about. In the past I would have allowed this sour coaching call with Flower Pop to wreck me, making it mean I'm garbage and I should quit coaching and teaching. Instead I decided I had done my best, and it probably was just a quiet group.

I practiced tuning in, allowing myself to feel shook, but then decided to not make a story of it, or make it mean more than that. I decided to follow relief and joy, and believe my best was enough.

I emailed the CEO and told her the call had an odd vibe, but maybe I was being sensitive! I asked if she wanted to review the call footage. I had presented the ideas she had deemed important, but I said maybe there was something I missed and could she let me know if there was something I could do to make it better or more effective for her team.

I let it go. I focused on my mastermind group for Thursday. I let Wednesday die. I jumped back in the river of flow.

Thursday's online mastermind group went awesome. It was fun, exciting, and full of the most wonderful humans. I got home Thursday, exhausted after six hours of nonstop engaging, listening, and teaching to a computer screen.

I watched a movie with my kids. In my old life, this would have never happened. I'd be too drained and beating myself up analyzing if everything I did that day was enough. I'd be wrapped up alone in a corner combing through every facial expression and word I'd said to make sure it was okay. Simply watching a movie with my kids is a huge freaking accomplishment for me. It's me flowing in the river of joy. Trusting that what I showed up with was the best I could do. And that I showed up with love, and intention to expand and share, and not control. Flow.

At 9 p.m. on Thursday I opened my email. I saw a response from Flower Pop's CEO and opened it. In a tone unlike any other communication I had ever received, it said I was terminated immediately, that I had brought no value, and while I was fun, I was lacking any substance. She told me they had received significant negative feedback, and that they had to dissolve the contract for nonperformance and ineffective coaching. There was more. But you get the idea.

To me it felt like she had called Satan himself and said, *Hey, what exact words could I use to hurt this woman the most? What are her deepest insecurities and how can I make sure to call them out and confirm them?*

I collapsed to the ground and started shaking. Eric, not sure what had happened, tried to talk to me but I could not speak. I started hyperventilating and crying. My kids walked out, scared and worried. Eric took them to their rooms. I rushed into the backyard and started screaming. How would we pay our rent? How would I go on after this? I thought of the thousands of students I'd sold courses to and had at my workshops. All I could think was, *She's right. I have no value. What do I do now? We'll have no income.*

I screamed so much I lost my voice. Eric came out and I tried to explain. But I finally just had to hand him my phone. The next morning was Friday and I had another all-day coaching session with my mastermind group. How was I supposed to show up to that, after this? I sobbed and sobbed and could barely catch my breath.

But here's what happened. In this pain, in this complete and total breakdown, joy guided me. Mind you, it didn't feel like joy, it felt like hell. But joy, God, my awesome inner knowing, it stayed with me through it all.

I was guided to get some medication. *Sleep, you getting sleep tonight is the only thing to focus on, let the rest go.* I also heard the direction: *Call Julie.*

At the time, Julie was my lone team member, and my person. She'd understand. I texted her a photo of the email, and then called her.

She immediately said, "I need you to hear me, I know it's hard. But I am here, living my dream, doing the work I want to do because of what you teach."

I had forgotten in that moment that Julie attended my very first Build an Awesome Brand workshop. I never forgot her and years later she was brought back into my life when I needed her the most. She moved her family across the country to help me do the work we're doing, she believes in it that much. This book, my work, it's not possible without her.

I heard Julie. That is a miracle. Being able to hear when you're in that state is a miracle. I slowed my breathing.

If Julie can believe, I will believe, just for now, I thought.

Later that night, I got a text message from my sister, Andrea. I had wanted her to join the mastermind session to help some of my product-focused students, but I had forgotten to text her and confirm. At almost midnight she texted out of the blue to ask, "Did you need me in the morning?"

Another miracle. I told her I needed her desperately. And gave her the schedule. She had someone who had flown in for a job interview, but he was going to have to wait.

I woke up the next morning and was still in shock. I looked in the mirror and said this, "You might be a fraud. You might be absolute crap as a coach. You might have no substance. So what? It means nothing about you. You are awesome. You are light. You are a child of God. That's all that matters."

I leaned into my vanity mirror deeper, "What's your intention? Love? Light? Yes? Okay. These people you're talking to today are yours to share love and light with today. God tasked you to do it. Period. Go do it. Let the rest go."

Another miracle.

Andrea brought the fun, enthusiastic energy to our first session and to me that was desperately needed. Miracles. I was able to be present, in the flow, and share love with my incredible students all day. Miracles. Out of the blue an old corporate coaching client texted me in the middle of the day. I had not heard from them in months. She said, "Just watching some of the training videos we did with you, you're incredible. We love working with you!"

Miracles. Each of these miracles were stepping-stones joy put in my path. Choosing them over my own low-level thoughts is what years of deciding to believe in my awesomeness helped me do.

In the middle of the day on Friday I got a text message from one of my contacts at Flower Pop. She wanted to talk. Instead of agonizing, I stayed present. After a joyous successful day of coaching, I called her back.

Immediately she said, "The CEO is so embarrassed. She didn't mean any of what she said. We want to hire you back."

Let that sink in. *Oops! Sorry! Never mind.*

The craziest thing is that when I read the email Thursday night at 9 p.m., my initial response, the response from the witness, not from my ego, had been, *These aren't her words, she's going to regret this.* But of course I thought those were the words of a delusional, self-important egomaniac. It's so hard to tell!

But because of that feeling I really had no malice at all toward the CEO. I immediately forgave her. Not because that's what "a good person does" or because it's how I hoped to feel. I genuinely felt it.

And shortly after, I received a beautiful heartfelt apology from the CEO.

The most unbelievable part of this story for me is that I felt okay, I carried on and believed in joy, before the "JUST KIDDING, you're not garbage!" phone call. That's the biggest miracle of all.

Long story not short, but shortened, the silent corporate executive on my coaching call was furious I had been hired. He was in charge of training and didn't want me involved. I was a big paycheck and big paychecks can ruffle big feathers—lesson learned. He'd been tearing me down for months to that small group of top leaders I had coached, and after that call on

Wednesday, the one I felt such weird vibes about but dismissed, he asked a couple of them to write emails saying basically "Alison sucks!" He wrote the email to fire me for the CEO and told her to push send. She regretted it immediately.

The best part is that maybe the only time in my life I decided to believe that people didn't hate me, they really did! But me believing that they did or didn't hate me changed nothing, except how I was able to show up for my life.

Some people in that small group did dislike me. They did think I was worthless as a coach and possibly as a human. And I chose to love myself all the same. I choose to love them all the same! They can't do anything about it.

Joy Is Your Purpose

One of the many reasons I love working with people on their dreams, their work, their lives, is because I get to show them they don't have to change anything they are doing to live their purpose. They didn't miss the call!

We often think our purpose is outside of us, hiding in a different career, a different partner, a different body, or some vague future version of yourself. But your purpose is the fuller expansion and understanding of your true core self. It's tapping into the reality of your limitlessness, your awesome, your life force energy that's coursing through you always! Joy will always call you to your purpose.

And your purpose calls to you in everything you do. It invites you to feel it as you do the dishes, saying, *Be here now!* As you clean up your bedroom and realize, *I have everything I need!* Your purpose beckons you when you let down your defenses and realize, *That hurtful thing my partner said has nothing to do with me. They are hurt, how can I have more understanding and be less judgmental?* Love, light, flow, surrender—this is your purpose! Your purpose always invites you into a fuller feeling of connection, creation, and expansion.

Think about it! God, the Universe, energy, nature, life, love, creativity, they want you to be BIG in the service of them. Not big like you dominate and are better than others, but big as in the awesome in you honors and sees the awesome in all other creations. That's big.

Our purpose is universal even if the words we use to define it are not. But how we express our purpose, our awesomeness, is unique to us. Unique to who we are! Not limited by who we are! Do you hear that? Our purpose is uniquely expressed by our talents, skills, life experience, circumstances, interests, and desires. Not limited by them!

Remember the shift *Joy has big plans for me!* Joy invites you to be big. When life feels too dark, too uncertain, and too confusing to plan on and plan for, that's the perfect time to sit still and look for what joy is trying to tell you, or listen to what it's calling you to feel or share. The needed talents and skills for your mission will unfold to you day by day as you continue to choose what lights you up, what calls you to joy.

The Next Best Thought

If I could go back to past versions of myself, to the girl smacking her head against her bedroom wall, or the girl pregnant and depressed, or the girl looking at a balcony to jump off because she made naive mistakes that offended others, I'd tell her, *It's okay.*

Feel this pain, let it make your heart beautiful. But don't forget, joy has big plans for you.

Each time you choose a thought, a belief, an action that expands and stretches you, to be more understanding, more compassionate, and feel some relief, you're choosing the next best thought. It doesn't always FEEL the best, like when we need to feel our painful feelings, make something right, acknowledge mistakes, or forgive someone who hurt us. But that pain is taking you on the right path. It's leading you back to joy.

When in doubt about what the next best thought is, TAP it out! Tune in, accept, and pick your focus. Which focus will lead you to joy? To relief, to peace? It might be you need help, therapy, medication, or counseling. It might be you need to have a conversation with a friend, apologize to someone, or forgive yourself. Your inner knowing always calls to you with joy, never with shame.

And the ultimate giver of relief is the knowledge that you are not these thoughts, you are not this form. You are SO MUCH BIGGER. You are pure joy.

Don't Miss Your Beautiful Life

The other day I desperately requested that Eric drive with me—meaning he drives and I ride shotgun—to do the kids' school drop-off. When we pulled up to preschool, Fiona also demanded that Eric escort her to the door. He is greatly loved. So I sat in the truck as he scooped her up, in her impossibly adorable green plaid jacket, and whisked her off.

She was so proud, so safe, so loved, so present to revel in the rare attention of both parents staring adoringly at her. And she kept reaching her arms out, while perched in her daddy's arms headed into preschool, waving and blowing me kisses with a dramatic flair that makes my heart soar.

This is my beautiful life, I thought to myself.

But the reason I hadn't just done the school drop-off alone like a normal functioning adult is because I barely felt like one. It seemed impossible. I was so anxious about my book deadline (this book) that I could barely peel myself out of bed. I woke up at 4 a.m. breathless and gasping with the exact thoughts, *Everyone hates you and is judging you. You are not qualified to write a book, you have no right to, you will be ripped apart. Your view is too narrow; no one needs a book from you.*

I focused on my breath and tried to slow my heart rate down. In the past I would have just stayed in bed. And sometimes I still do. I wanted to burrow into the sheets, build a nest, and never leave. My bed is safe. No one hates me in my bed, or if they do, I don't have to know about it. But rather than forcing myself up early to exercise or belittling myself for slipping into negative, ungrateful thoughts, I just kept choosing to believe, *It might all be true, and you're still okay. It might all be true, but right now let's just try to live this beautiful life.*

I hoped that by getting out of bed, even if I couldn't face doing it alone, it would at least keep me from spiraling. I made a conscious effort to try to stay present with my children as we dropped them off. I chose joy over and over and over.

I watched my ten- and seven-year-olds, in masks, trudge into a school day that is currently wildly different from what they used to experience or from what they would choose. Giant backpacks eclipsing their tiny bodies. They are so brave. They are so brilliant and resilient. They are my example of continuing to choose joy. And so I do.

See, the thing is there's always a reason to miss our beautiful lives. There will always be another problem to solve unless we decide to stop trying to solve problems and just flow and observe. There's always something to figure out, someone else's feelings about us to try to dissect. There's always someone who might fire us and tell us all the things we hoped we'd never hear. But you're exactly where you need to be, you get to show up as you are, right now, and you're being guided and supported as you do.

Don't miss your beautiful life.

It's right in front of your eyes. It's in your heart, it's all right here. Your beautiful life is not devoid of suffering or panic or fear. Your beautiful life is not the published book that no one rips apart, or the weight lost, or the job gained, the partner secured, the child successful and safe. Your beautiful life is the day-to-day unfolding of all the little pieces, feelings, and parts of the whole reflecting back to you the beauty of this earth.

The child who feels loved and secure enough to wave with dramatic queenlike flair as she's carried off to preschool. The husband who drives me around even when it makes no logical sense.

So when people shout, "Gratitude!" "Presence!" "Focus on the good!," they're really just saying, "Don't miss your beautiful life!" Because you will if you keep thinking that the beauty has to be devoid of pain or fear.

Nothing has to change for everything to be different. Nothing has to be checked off, accomplished, earned, or proven for you to feel like you've made it. In fact, I spend hours and hours talking to people who have achieved every possible goal they set out to get and still feel empty, not enough.

Throughout this entire book, I've been telling you to believe, to have faith, that you are already awesome. You don't need to do anything, change anything, listen to anyone—you are inherently and wholly awesome. Right now. You just need to awaken to it. And it turns out that being awesome looks like having a beautiful life.

The secret is this: This is your beautiful life right now. You can work to feel it or not. But nothing outside of you will create it. If you are unable to feel it, that's okay. Noticing you are unable to feel it is an incredibly powerful step. So let me ask you this, do you believe you are worthy of feeling your beautiful life?

If the answer is yes, which I hope it is, then what help or assistance or guidance do you need so that you can feel again? A course? A doctor? A chat with a friend?

If more of us with beautiful lives, with basic needs met, and resources flowing felt worthy of feeling our beautiful lives, even with their pain and heartbreak, we'd have more energy and time to spend looking for ways to help others secure beautiful lives.

Your beautiful, imperfect, awesome life is a terrible thing to waste. Don't miss your beautiful life.

The Year of Magical Peeing

Don't blame yourself, and don't ask why.
That's the art of getting by.

—LAURA ZOCCA

After turning in my first draft in December of 2020, my health took a sharp decline. Fresh off writing this book, fresh off needing to tap into unconditional love every day in order to write, I finally, after thirty-plus years of ignoring, pushing down, or being too busy for certain pain, watched it surface.

At first it wasn't too physical, but I did feel very run down. I felt a dark fog creeping over my shoulder at first. A shadow on my right side just as the draft was being finished up. I wasn't afraid of the shadow, but it did have a sort of inevitable feeling around it. Like it was something I had been avoiding that I no longer could avoid. It was the first time I had ever been able to identify, believe, and allow the feeling, the sense. That there was something dark inside me to face, to meet, to understand. The shadow self, as Jung would say. And then my body began to shut down.

Dutiful writer, teacher, and human that I am, I did what I wrote in this book! I would tune in, accept the pain—physical, blearing, mind-altering pain—and then pick. I would pick my focus, and with so much physical pain, unable to pee for days, unable to stop peeing other days. The pain led to ER trips, I passed a gallstone, fought infection, and nothing they did or tried brought relief. I watched as I was filled with shame that I was STILL in pain—STILL not okay month after month. Again and again I had to choose to focus on accepting my pain. I worked to not judge it. Not to force it to be something better or more acceptable.

It.

Was.

So.

Hard.

My beautiful life had become too painful to live in. And, sometimes, it still feels that way.

It's been the type of year where for months I was too sick to walk to the kitchen; I'm in too much pain to drive or leave bed many days. It's been the type of year where every single specialist of every sort tells me something different. I believe it will resolve; I believe solutions are already in place. I believe. I choose with difficulty, but I choose to believe this physical reality is not my new normal. But I am also exhausted. I thought surely, SURELY, by the time it was time to finish the book, I would be healed.

I am not, yet. But I am able to do all that is needed, at the time it is needed.

I've spent more hours crying in the bathroom, in the car, on the side of walking trails, and curled up in a ball in pain in front of strangers than I would ever wish on any person. Except maybe a few. Oh see, I let my inner Ursula out! Poor, unfortunate souls.

I have spent hours, days, nights, just so mad at God and seeking to know a Goddess (who became a HUGE part of my healing, a feminine Divine)—and begging both to end my suffering. I spent an equal amount of time deciding I wasn't being tough enough and to get over it.

Due to my health, I was unable to do events or work. I stopped posting on Instagram, something I had NEVER let myself do. I stopped pouring out. I stopped recording my podcast, and slowly, because I decided to honor my pain and listen to my body, I watched every revenue stream I had worked and fought and toiled for dry up. I kept thinking the wheel of fate would drop a financial lifeline. Nope. I watched my in-box get quiet and many, not all, but many, friends who had gotten used to me initiating the relationship faded quietly away.

I was too truly ill to leave bed for months, but it still felt like an impossible choice to stop doing and focus on my healing because I've never honored my own illness. I've never honored my pain to stop before I'm, well, hit by a car. (Only I get to make the joke!) And even then, I kind of only paused. It was the BEST I could do at the time.

But this book! I had to stay true to it and what it taught me as I wrote it. I could no longer force myself to be so harsh and ruthless on my body and psyche. I am already awesome.

When my last full-time employee, Julie, decided it was time for her to quit, so she could be my friend and not someone I paid to support me, I, to my own surprise and horror, understood and agreed with her. I needed her as a friend, she is still my dearest friend.

It no longer made sense for me to keep my office space, so the week after Julie quit I let my dream office—the one I had spent years building up, the one with the PERFECT wall color—go. In my physical pain, I had to repair and restore my vibrant office to an all-white studio. And while doing so I fell off a ladder and bruised my tailbone. I also had a bowel blockage that week. They were dark days.

The only thing I kept up and running was my community Awesome on Demand. At first only because I didn't have enough money to reimburse people to get out. But then it became a lifeline, one place that I could share and declare, "I STILL BELIEVE. In me. I believe in myself. I believe I am worthy of sharing. That I am allowed to share. I believe it still might work out, it won't always be THIS hard, let's believe together."

In many low moments I hoarsely choked out threats to God through my sobs. After a searing jolt of pain would render me gobsmacked, and crying while clutching my intestines yet again, I would become incensed. "HAVEN'T I GIVEN ENOUGH?! HAVEN'T I SUFFERED AND BLED AND SACRIFICED ENOUGH? I WILL NOT DO ANYMORE!"

I often have to pee nearly forty times a day. It can make me start to feel batty, as doing something repetitive that interrupts and demands attention does. But my newest habit while healing is asking, "What's the kindest, most compassionate response or action I could take?"

One day I asked myself this question, climbed into a bath, sobbed while listening to choir music, and then sat in a comfy chair to stare blankly at the wall. That was the kindest thing I could do. Not look for answers or a positive thought.

As I stared at nothing in particular a book caught my eye that I had bought a few months earlier. I sat in my chair and read the book in its entirety. It's only eighty pages, but in *She* Jungian analyst Robert A. Johnson breaks down and gives insight on the ancient myth of Aphrodite and Psyche. This sentence immediately filled me with hope:

> Almost always in human experience the urge toward
> suicide signals an edge of a new level of consciousness.
> If you can kill the right thing—the old way of
> adaptation—and not injure yourself, a new energy-
> filled era will begin.[17]

It's been a year of massive pain, loss, sadness, and anger. A year of nonstop peeing. But also a year of magic.

In the great beyond, as we watch the days of our lives replayed, I think we will focus much less on what we accomplished and just marvel at all we survived, all we forgave. The miracles that got us through. I want to look back in awe at what I continued to believe in, what I continued to believe was possible, even when the evidence felt contrary.

I don't have a conclusion that sums up everything in this book and in my life thus far nicely. But I do have a testimony. A testimony of living what I have written. It has transformed me.

Parts of me that I thought had to be silenced have been given back their voice. Pieces of me that I thought were not acceptable and pleasing have surfaced. Not everyone is delighted, AND YET I TRUDGE FORTH!

I'm the girl with the million-dollar brand who let it all go to hell in order to heal. I'm the girl who bought nachos with car change for dinner last night.

It's tempting to believe answers are outside of us. We can spend our whole lives thinking other people know more and are more qualified to direct your life. But the truth is we GET to write our own conclusions. And other people, people who write books like me, or your parents or friends, or other people who are really good at communicating, never inherently know more or better for you than YOU.

I get to now offer this book and my words to you not so that I can sleep at night knowing I'm worthy of breathing. And not to further a career or plan for world domination. I offer it in humility. I offer it because I have it to offer. I no longer have some illusory sense of authority—I'm tired and I have to pee. But peace is my pearl of great price. And I am at peace. I strive for and long for even deeper peace that I can imperfectly show up and love myself unconditionally.

I am at peace that I am already as awesome as I need to be. And I'm really proud and grateful to scream, to shout, to whisper, and to live this truth:

Only you can be you. And you're already as awesome as you need to be.

ACKNOWLEDGMENTS

The reason I was able to write this book is because as I've opened up my heart, people have shared their lives and hearts with me. They shared their stories, their dreams, their fears. Thank you for this trust. Thank you for sharing your hearts, your light, your wisdom and support in so many ways.

My kids are a huge source of light and joy, as well as deeper understanding. Thank you Ginger for listening so sweetly, Rad for your Raddy Power, and Fiona for your fire. I love you to the moon and back.

I'm so lucky to know I am loved by my parents. Thank you to my mom and dad for fearlessly sharing with the world so I felt brave enough to as well. Mom, thank you for teaching me to love words and learning. Thank you for always telling me how brilliant I am and for all those conclusions you wrote for my essays in school. Dad, thank you for always encouraging me to dream even bigger and always be kind. And thank you for all your dance moves I've stolen.

Thank you to all the volunteers, artists, and humans over the past decade plus that have given their time and talent to help create my events and workshops. Thank you. If I was too anxious or stressed to thank you directly in the moment, please know that I often gasp in appreciation when I think of YOU. Thank you.

Thank you to the awesome, heartfelt team at HarperOne for making my dreams come true and for helping create this book. You chose the best words. I'm so grateful I didn't have to do it alone.

NOTES

1. Michael A. Singer, *The Untethered Soul: The Journey Beyond Yourself* (Oakland, CA: New Harbinger Publications, 2007).

2. Foundation for Inner Peace, *A Course in Miracles: Combined Volume* (Novato, CA: Foundation for Inner Peace, 2008).

3. Lao-Tzu, *Tao Te Ching* (New York: Harper Perennial, 1992).

4. Don Miguel Ruiz, *The Four Agreements: A Practical Guide to Personal Freedom* (New York: Random House, 1997).

5. M. W. Bos and A. Dijksterhuis, "Unconscious Thought Works Bottom-Up and Conscious Thought Works Top-Down When Forming an Impression," *Social Cognition* 29, no. 6 (2011): 727–37, https://psycnet.apa.org/record/2011-28859-008.

6. J. Pennebaker, "Your Use of Pronouns Reveals Your Personality," *Harvard Business Review* 89, no. 12 (2011): 32–33, https://hbr.org/2011/12/your-use-of-pronouns-reveals-your-personality.

7. Saundra Dalton-Smith, *Sacred Rest: Recover Your Life, Renew Your Energy, Restore Your Sanity* (New York: FaithWords, 2019).

8. Arthur O'Shaughnessy, "Ode," in *Music and Moonlight; Poems and Songs* (Hardpress Publishing, 2012).

9. *Moana*, directed by Ron Clements and John Musker (Los Angeles: Disney, 2016), film.

10. Bessel van der Kolk, *The Body Keeps the Score: Brain, Mind, and Body in the Healing of Trauma* (New York: Penguin Books, 2015).

11. Steven Stosny, "Changing Emotional Habits," *Psychology Today*, October 13, 2019: https://www.psychologytoday.com/us/blog/anger-in-the-age-entitlement/201910/changing-emotional-habits.

12. Katie Avis-Riordan, "There Are Actually 27 Human Emotions, New Study Finds," *Country Living*, September 11, 2017: https://www.countryliving.com/uk/wellbeing/news/a2454/27-human-emotions-new-study.

13. Lao-Tzu, *Tao Te Ching* (New York: Harper Perennial, 1992).

14. Seth Godin, "Qarrtsiluni," *Seth's Blog*, November 21, 2020, https://seths.blog/2020/11/qarrtsiluni.

15. Loch Kelly, *The Way of Effortless Mindfulness: A Revolutionary Guide for Living an Awakened Life* (Louisville, CO: Sounds True, 2019).

16. Nicole LePera, *How to Do the Work: Recognize Your Patterns, Heal from Your Past, and Create Your Self* (New York: HarperWave, 2021).

17. Robert A. Johnson, *She: Understanding Feminine Psychology* (New York: Harper Perennial, 2020).

WORKS CITED AND LOVED!

Bernstein, Gabrielle. *Judgment Detox: Release the Beliefs That Hold You Back from Living a Better Life*. New York: Gallery Books, 2018.

Bernstein, Gabrielle. *The Universe Has Your Back: Transform Fear to Faith*. New York: Random House, 2016.

Brown, Brené. *Dare to Lead: Brave Work. Tough Conversations. Whole Hearts*. New York: Random House, 2018.

Brown, Brené. *Daring Greatly: How the Courage to Be Vulnerable Transforms the Way We Live, Love, Parent, and Lead*. New York: Avery, 2015.

Brown, Brené. *The Power of Vulnerability: Teachings on Authenticity, Connection, and Courage*. Louisville, CO: Sounds True, 2013. Audiobook.

Dalton-Smith, Saundra. *Sacred Rest: Recover Your Life, Renew Your Energy, Restore Your Sanity*. New York: FaithWords, 2019.

Didion, Joan. *The Year of Magical Thinking*. New York: Random House, 2007.

Dyer, Wayne W. *Change Your Thoughts—Change Your Life: Living the Wisdom of the Tao*. Carlsbad, CA: Hay House, 2007.

Estés, Clarissa Pinkola. *Women Who Run with the Wolves: Myths and Stories of the Wild Woman Archetype*. New York: Ballantine Books, 1992.

Frankl, Viktor E. *Man's Search for Meaning*. Boston: Beacon Press, 2006.

Gilbert, Elizabeth. *Big Magic: Creative Living Beyond Fear*. New York: Penguin Books, 2016.

Godin, Seth. *This Is Marketing: You Can't Be Seen Until You Learn to See*. New York: Portfolio, 2018. Illustrated edition.

Hoff, Benjamin. *The Tao of Pooh*. New York: Penguin Books, 1983.

Homer, Nakeia. *I Hope This Helps*. Nakeia, 2020.

Kelly, Loch. *The Way of Effortless Mindfulness: A Revolutionary Guide for Living an Awakened Life.* Louisville, CO: Sounds True, 2019.

Kite, Lexie, and Lindsay Kite. *More Than a Body: Your Body Is an Instrument, Not an Ornament.* Boston: Houghton Mifflin Harcourt, 2020.

Ruiz, Don Miguel. *The Four Agreements: A Practical Guide to Personal Freedom.* San Rafael, CA: Amber-Allen Publishing, 2018.

Sincero, Jen. *You Are a Badass: How to Stop Doubting Your Greatness and Start Living an Awesome Life.* New York: Hachette, 2013.

Singer, Michael A. *The Surrender Experiment: My Journey into Life's Perfection.* New York: Harmony Books, 2015.

Singer, Michael A. *The Untethered Soul: The Journey Beyond Yourself.* Oakland, CA: New Harbinger Publications, 2007.

Singer, Michael A. *The Untethered Soul Lecture Series Collection, Volumes 1-4.* Louisville, CO: Sounds True, 2020. Audiobook.

Singer, Michael A. *The Untethered Soul Lecture Series Collection, Volumes 5-8.* Louisville, CO: Sounds True, 2020. Audiobook.

Tolle, Eckhart. *A New Earth: Awakening to Your Life's Purpose.* New York: Penguin Life, 2008.

Tolle, Eckhart. *The Power of Now: A Guide to Spiritual Enlightenment.* Novato, CA: New World Library, 1999.

van der Kolk, Bessel. *The Body Keeps the Score: Brain, Mind, and Body in the Healing of Trauma.* New York: Penguin Books, 2015.

Walker, Alice. *The Color Purple.* New York: Penguin Books, 2019.

Williamson, Marianne. *A Return to Love: Reflections on the Principles of A Course in Miracles.* New York: HarperOne, 1996.

Zukav, Gary. *The Seat of the Soul.* New York: Simon & Schuster, 2014. Revised edition.